The Media Players

The Media Players

Shakespeare, Middleton, Jonson, and the Idea of News

STEPHEN WITTEK

University of Michigan Press
Ann Arbor

Published in the United States of America by the
University of Michigan Press
Manufactured in the United States of America
♾ Printed on acid-free paper

2018 2017 2016 2015 4 3 2 1

A CIP catalog record for this book is available from the British Library.

Library of Congress Cataloging-in-Publication Data

Wittek, Stephen.
The media players : Shakespeare, Middleton, Jonson, and the idea of news / Stephen Wittek.
pages cm
Includes bibliographical references and index.
ISBN 978-0-472-07281-1 (hardcover : acid-free paper) —
ISBN 978-0-472-05281-3 (pbk. : acid-free paper) —
ISBN 978-0-472-12134-2 (ebook)
1. English drama—Early modern and Elizabethan, 1500–1600—History and criticism. 2. Journalism—England—History—16th century. 3. Mass media and literature—Great Britain—History. 4. Theater and society—England—History—16th century. 5. English drama—17th century—History and criticism. 6. Theater and society—England—History—17th century. I. Title.

PR651.W55 2015
822'.309355—dc23

2015000676

Acknowledgments

The research for this book was carried out with support from the Social Sciences and Humanities Research Council of Canada, the Shakespeare Institute at the University of Birmingham, the Department of English at McGill University, and the Institute for the Public Life of Arts and Ideas (McGill). Some of the material in chapter 3 derives from an essay for the Spring 2015 edition of the journal *Studies in English Literature*. Sincere thanks to the many colleagues who have provided help and guidance along the way: Paul Yachnin, Richard Dutton, Wes Folkerth, Kate McLuskie, John Jowett, Joshua McEvilla, Kenneth Borris, and John Munro. In the summer of 2014, the CBC Radio One program *Ideas* aired an episode that provides an excellent hour-long introduction to my research.[1] Many thanks to the producers, Tom Howell and Nicola Luksic, and to the scholars who offered commentary on the work: Ann Cvetkovich, Andrew Pettegree, and Paul Yachnin (who is richly deserving of double thanks). On a personal note, I also want to thank my mother, Coleen Wittek, my grandparents, Dorothy and Samuel Close, and, above all, my very gracious and savvy wife, Heejung Yoon—this accomplishment is as much hers as it is mine (사랑해요). Finally, I want to thank my son, William Wittek, and my daughter, Lily Wittek. To be honest, neither of you were any help at all, but you provided limitless joy and comfort, making the labor of writing much more enjoyable than any scholar might reasonably expect.

Contents

CHAPTER 1

Early Modern Drama and the Idea of News

This book builds a case for the central, formative function of Shakespeare's theater in the news culture of early modern England. In an analysis that combines literary criticism with historical research and recent developments in public sphere theory, I argue that the unique discursive space created by commercial theater helped to foster the conceptual framework that made news possible. On this view, the animating force behind the emergence of news culture lies, not only with the development of new technologies and trade routes, but also with the groundbreaking cultural developments that gave rise to the sophisticated idea of "the news" itself, an idea that I define as the distinctly modern notion of ephemeral, narratively structured, ostensibly truthful discourse standing in relation to a continuous, public present. In other words, my analysis puts emphasis on the coevolution of material innovations and the equally innovative development of the *concept* of news itself—thereby offering an alternative to histories that explain modern news culture as a predetermined corollary of advances in print technology alone. News was not a latent phenomenon just waiting for print to come along and make it happen, nor was it an idea wholly constituted by print media. Rather, the growth of news-related thinking derived force and direction from various interconnected forms of publicity, theater in particular.

The unique role theater played in the development of news hinges on the distinctive position it took up in regard to topicality and the truth.

Unlike other means of representing current events, theatrical discourse did not present itself as true—it depended for effect on a knowing disengagement from reality, an implicit awareness that Burbage was not really Richard III and the Globe Theatre was not really Bosworth Field. Compounding this formal barrier to reality, dramatists of the period typically approached topical concerns from an oblique angle, or from behind the guise of a sophisticated conceit, thus making the connection to news a matter of imaginative interpretation, or play. Paradoxically, however, such techniques did not fence the theater off from news culture but in fact made it a unique space where formative thinking about the news could flourish, a space where the *concept* of news could become manifest from an elucidating distance and could accrue value in an emotionally and intellectually resonant register. This study tracks that development in an analysis of three plays from 1611 to 1626: Shakespeare's *A Winter's Tale* (perf. 1611), Middleton's *A Game at Chess* (perf. 1624), and Jonson's *The Staple of News* (perf. 1626). To put these readings in perspective, the first chapter will articulate a clear definition of what the idea of news entails and sketch out a brief history of how it took hold in the seventeenth century.

Theater and News Culture: A Brief History

The origin of commercial theater in England predates the beginning of commercial news culture by about fifteen years. In 1576, James Burbage constructed the first building for exclusively theatrical purposes in the London suburb of Shoreditch, thereby inaugurating an industry that quickly grew to sustain multiple professional acting companies and a wide variety of venues. Theater historian Andrew Gurr estimates that in the years between the 1560s and 1642, as many as 2,500 people went to London theaters every week, for a total of approximately fifty million visits—a remarkable rate of attendance for a population that ranged from 200,000 to 350,000 during the period.[1] Commercial news culture developed more gradually, beginning around the mid-sixteenth century with the occasional publication of inexpensive pamphlets, then gaining momentum in the 1590s with John Wolfe's semiregular (but short-lived) series of translated news quartos specializing in reports on the French wars (the popularity of these documents corresponds to the period of England's involvement in the conflict).[2] Around the same time, a steady market also developed for inexpensive pamphlets recounting events such as natural disasters, mysterious births, and sensational murders. Nearly 450 publications of this sort appeared between 1591 and 1610, accounting for a quarter of all items entered in the Stationer's Register.[3] As the seventeenth century progressed, a growing news consciousness gave rise to a number of systematized and informal mechanisms for circulating information: "newsmongers" congregated at the gossip shop around St. Paul's Cathedral, peddlers sold news texts in the streets, patrons sang broadside ballads posted on tavern walls, and professional news services made manuscript newsletters available to subscribers throughout the country. In the early 1620s, Nathaniel Butter and a group of fellow printers and publishers formed England's first news syndicate, an extensive operation that specialized in the publication of inexpensive translations of foreign newssheets known as corantos. Produced on a regular basis for popular consumption (like commercial drama), the corantos made news a routine commodity, a readily available staple of the Jacobean economy. The codification of this commercial foothold made news and drama partners in a common cause. Both forms were essentially selling the same product—narrative configurations—to the same popular audience, and both helped to establish a new culture of ongoing public conversation, a culture where news could be a salable product.

Theater functioned as a part of news culture in a number of respects, but most prominently by way of allegory or subtle reference to current events. A well-known example is the Porter's speech on equivocation in *Macbeth*, which is probably an allusion to the trial of the Jesuit Henry Garnet on 28 March 1606.[4] In other instances, a dramatist might build on the imagery and interest surrounding a prominent news story, as Shakespeare did when he drew on material from William Strachey's account of a 1609 shipwreck to write *The Tempest*.[5] On rare occasions, the theater could also bring printed pamphlets to life on stage. Such was the case with *The Yorkshire Tragedy*, a 1608 dramatization of a pamphlet about an English squire who stabbed his wife and murdered two of his children. Another important example is *Sir John van Olden Barnavelt*, a play about the execution of a Dutch statesman that came out a mere 104 days after the actual execution occurred.[6] Adaptations along these lines were uncommon, however, because, despite its appeal, topical representation carried a considerable risk. The default attitude of authority toward professional drama was generally dismissive, but companies could get in serious trouble for material that touched the reputations of public men.[7] For example, in 1605, Ben Jonson found himself imprisoned and (purportedly) at risk of losing his nose and ears for writing a satire on Scots that came a little too close to disparaging the Scottish king. Four years later, a similar offense in a satire by John Marston provoked the official disbandment of an entire theatrical company. To avoid outcomes such as these, dramatists typically transferred the underlying ideas of news stories to an entirely separate narrative—a technique that made topicality a matter of interpretation rather than explicit exposition.[8] For example, consider the four "disguised prince" dramas that appeared around the time of James I's ascension to the throne: Marston's *The Malcontent* (1603), Middleton's *The Phoenix* (1603), Day's *Law-Tricks* (1604), and Shakespeare's *Measure for Measure* (1604).[9] All of these plays feature a ruler who assumes a disguise in order to view society as it appears from the perspective of ordinary subjects. In each case, this plot device leads to the discovery of corruption and a meditation on issues related to judicious governance, thereby extending and enriching a conversation ongoing in news culture about how the new monarch ought to go about the business of ruling England. In addition to re-mediating news discourse in this manner, the theater also offered critical analysis of the news industry itself, a task that Ben Jonson took up with gusto throughout his career—most notably in *The Staple of News,* one of the most thoughtful and comprehensive critiques of news culture from the period. In yet other instances, theatrical productions actually became the subject of news, as was the case with Middleton's *A Game at Chess,* a play that channeled news discourse surrounding Prince Charles's trip to Spain, but also caused enough of a stir to become a news event itself. Such cases testify to the fluid, symbiotic relationship between news and drama. Theater did not merely reflect or repackage news narratives—it was a dynamic, influential component of the overall news culture.

Theatergoing also offered patrons an exciting physical closeness to news. If one were lucky, the price of admission to a dramatic production could buy proximity to living newsmakers. Notable persons such as ambassadors and nobles occasionally exhibited their magnificence from prestige seats in the balcony or onstage, providing an added layer of spectacle for the crowds below. As one of Jonson's meta-spectators notes in the induction to *The Staple of News,* people went to the theater "to see and to be seen" (7), to participate in an environment of mutual public display. Facilitated by the circular design and dense occupancy of London's early theaters, this unique concentration of nonexclusive, intensely social activity created a natural news hub, a place where people could go to disseminate and discuss issues of topical concern. The opportunities that such a space presented for the circulation of news become particularly apparent in light of three manuscript newsletter accounts of a notable appearance at the Globe by the Duke of Buckingham, one of the most powerful men in England at the time.[10] Besieged by accusations of corruption and incompetence following a series of increasingly disastrous missteps, Buckingham attended a revival of Fletcher and Shakespeare's *Henry VIII* in early August 1628 and caused a considerable stir by leaving after the first scene in the second act—the point at which the character Buckingham, a loyal servant of the King, loses his head as the result of a smear campaign orchestrated by the malevolent counselor, Cardinal Wolsey. No one can be sure about the precise intention motivating this conspicuously timed exit, but the reaction it provoked says a good deal about the news-relevancy accredited to theatrical meaning. For example, consider the description of the event by the professional newsletter writer Robert Gell:

> On teusday his Grace was present at y[e] acting of K. Hen 8 at y[e] Globe, a play bespoken of purpose by himself; whereat he stayd till y[e] Duke of Buckingham was beheaded, & then departed. Some say, he should rather have seen y[e] fall of Cardinall Woolsey, who was a more lively type of himself, having governed this kingdom 18 yeares, as he had done 14.

The implicit assumption behind Gell's account of the incident is that Buckingham wanted the audience to perceive some sort of connection between popular rumor and the events of the play. Regardless of whether or not this was actually the case, the report shows that people were not unaccustomed to attaching topical significance to theatrical fiction. Tellingly, some observers apparently understood the news parallel, but offered their own interpretation, suggesting the villain Wolsey was a better analogue for Buckingham ("a more lively type of himself") than his innocent namesake presented onstage. As Thomas Cogswell and Peter Lake argue in a recent essay, the duke quite likely orchestrated the entire event, including the revival of the play itself (which was fifteen years old by that point).[11] This possibility seems particularly likely when one considers the limited channels for public communication available at the time. Jacobean England did not have an equivalent of news interview shows, or any other mass forum where public figures could go to respond to rumor. As Andrew Gurr notes, the theater was "the only major medium for social intercommunication, the only existing form of journalism and the only occasion that existed for the gathering of large numbers of people other than for sermons and executions."[12] In other words, theater was something like a default news platform, one of the only physical spaces where an informal large-scale, live broadcast could take place.[13]

Gurr's description of the theater as "the only existing form of journalism" requires some qualification, however. Interpreted narrowly, the statement is quite simply untrue: journalism did not really exist at all, either as an idea or as an industry, until the 1620s, and even then only in a rather rudimentary sense. As noted above, the concept of "news" itself was only beginning to gain traction in the period—the systematic practice of investigating, reporting, editing, fact checking, and publishing that underlies the profession of journalism would not begin to take hold in a substantial way until the English Civil War. But, of course, this is precisely Gurr's point: in the absence of a comprehensive mechanism for reporting and publicizing information, the activities of London's theatrical companies amounted to something like a de facto press, a loosely organized network of independent producers in the business of transmitting various types of information, including (but not necessarily limited to) news. Gurr probably pushes the idea a bit too far by describing theater as "the *only* existing form of journalism" (if drama counts as journalism, then surely topical ballads, manuscript newsletters, and printed pamphlets would have to count as well), but his general point about the unparalleled power of the theater to make information public is certainly correct. To get a full sense of this power, one must take into account the tremendous reach that dramatic discourse commanded. First, as an oral, visual medium, drama could speak directly to the vast number of people who were unable to read, a capability that allowed access to a far larger potential audience than printed (or written) forms of publication could ever hope to attain.[14] Second, in addition to attracting a steady audience to London's twenty or so venues, theatrical companies regularly performed at court, in the private homes of wealthy patrons, and at various guildhalls, monasteries, castles, and other civic centers throughout England.[15] This remarkable range of social and geographic movement established an information network that encompassed the entirety of English society—everyone from swineherds, to tradesmen, to courtiers, to the king himself. As Gurr's comments suggest, such a network resembles journalism, not only in terms of substance, but also in terms of structure: it established a platform for social intercommunication that journalism would build on and help to codify in the coming centuries. This similarity between the two forms suggests the early modern theater played a much more important role in the eighteenth-century transformation of public life than Jürgen Habermas's theory of the public sphere allows. I will have much more to say about Habermas presently, but before I move from historical context to theory there is one further important area of overlap between drama and news to bring into the picture: printed playtexts.

Performance space was not the only point of contact between theater and news. Drama also maintained a minor, but steady foothold in print culture, primarily in the form of inexpensive quartos sold alongside the news pamphlets and other literature that lined the bookstalls at St. Paul's. In many cases, dramatic quartos were merely a sideline for publishers specializing in more straightforwardly topical forms of literature. For example, Nathaniel Butter, one of the founders of England's first news syndicate (and the specific target of much of the satire in *The Staple of News*), published a number of dramatic texts over his long career, including Dekker's *The Whore of Babylon* (perf. 1606, pub. 1607) and Shakespeare's *King Lear* (perf. 1605, pub. 1608). Publications such as these facilitated the diffusion of dramatic discourse from public performance spaces to the more private areas of society, thereby extending the reach and influence of the theatrical information network. In addition, the malleable valance of dramatic texts meant that the act of publication itself could sometimes reconstitute an old play's relevance to news discourse, just as the Duke of Buckingham reconstituted the topical relevance of *Henry VIII* by bringing it into dialogue with rumors circulating in the late 1620s. As a groundbreaking study by Zachary Lesser has shown, publishers would often plot intersections between news and drama quite purposefully in order to cultivate a market around a particular area of specialization. One of his primary examples of this tactic is the case of Thomas Archer, a publisher who specialized in literature that addressed (and cultivated) contemporary debate over the proper role of women in society. Archer practiced what Lesser calls "dialogic publishing": the strategy of bringing out publications from opposed viewpoints in order to foster debate around a particular issue. In 1615, a prospective customer browsing around Archer's shop in Pope's Head Alley (near the Royal Exchange) might see Joseph Swetnam's *Araignment of Lewde, Idle, Froward, and Unconstant Women* (London, 1615), Rachel Speght's vigorous rebuttal, *A Mouzell for Melastomus, the Cynical Bayter of, and Foule Mouthed Barker Against Euahs Sex* (London, 1616), and a handful of plays that offered a dramatic perspective on the same theme: Middleton and Rowley's *The Roaring Girl* (perf. 1611, pub. 1611), Webster's *The White Devil* (perf. 1612, pub. 1612), and Marston's *The Insatiate Countess* (perf.

1607, pub. 1613).[16] Another example along the same lines is the case of Thomas Walkley, a publisher who specialized in literature related to parliamentary affairs, but also brought out a handful of playtexts—most notably, the first quarto of Shakespeare's *Othello* (1622). Lesser argues that in Walkley's hands, *Othello,* a play written by Shakespeare in 1604, came into dialogue with the news discourse of 1622: "In *Othello,* Walkley's readers—and members of Parliament, we know, were among them—could see enacted both the fears of mercenaries expressed in the 1621 parliament and the accompanying desire for a more chivalric and 'Elizabethan' mode of warfare, a holy war against Spain and Rome."[17] As with the account of Buckingham's visit to the Globe, examples such as these help to bring the topical relevancy of drama into perspective. By enabling people to think through current events in an interconnected, analytical, familiar, and emotional manner, theatrical discourse assisted at the birth of one of the most important concepts in the history of literature: the idea of news.

The Idea of News

As noted in the introduction to this chapter, the present study defines the idea of news as "the distinctly modern notion of ephemeral, narratively structured, ostensibly truthful discourse standing in relation to a continuous, public present." This definition will require some careful unpacking, beginning with "distinctly modern." The familiar ubiquity and fundamental position of news in contemporary society make it easy to overlook the fact that there was once a time when the very idea of news was inchoate and strikingly new. Recapturing a sense of this intense, uncertain newness is essential to understanding the historical transformation of news in early modernity. Of course, any history of news has to begin by acknowledging that certain aspects of the phenomenon were never really new at all. Basic practices of dispersing information among individuals and groups are fundamental to any functioning society and presumably date back to the beginning of civilization, but the idea of "the news" that began to develop in the seventeenth century goes a good deal beyond mere information sharing. For example, it involves a notion of spatiality. Consider the conceptual underpinning of phrases such as "in the news," or "out of the news." The space that such phrases refer to is not merely a newspaper, radio broadcast, or even a combination of media. Rather, it is a public, a discursive space constituted by common awareness, open to anyone inclined to pay attention. The idea of news also involves a notion of shared time: it posits a temporality that bridges the near past and the absolute present, creating a public sense of simultaneous experience, a sense that people in multiple, disparate locations can have access to an event that is happening "now."

I will have more to say about spatiality and temporality later on, but for the moment I simply want to submit these features as examples that demonstrate the distinctly modern nature of news. Modern, that is, not only because of their complexity, but also because of their affinity to the broadened worldview and increased opportunities for social interaction that characterize early modernity. The idea of news is distinctly modern, in other words, because it operates according to the logic of a modern epistemology, a way of knowing rooted in an assumption of one's place within a vast, interconnected world.

The notion of a public "now" created by news connects to the next distinguishing feature in my definition: ephemerality. The news is in a constant state of flux, always opening into the present at one end and receding into obscurity at the other. No single item can ever remain "in the news" for long before it yields to items of greater currency. This fundamental impermanency is central to the way news establishes value. "Looke your Newes be new, and fresh," warns Gossip Tattle at the beginning of Jonson's *The Staple of News*. "I shall find them else, if they be stale, or flye-blowne quickly" (Induction 25–27). Tattle's warning is the first stroke in an analogy to food that Jonson develops throughout the play. In his world and our own, news is a perishable commodity, and as such its value decreases as it moves away from the present. In this sense, ephemerality is a value-enhancing property: our knowledge that news will not stay new forever makes it all the more precious at the point of reception. On the other hand, however, ephemerality also makes news vulnerable to charges of frivolity. Jonson's food analogy exploits this weakness by suggesting that news is no more than a fashionable excuse for chatter—a titillating but insubstantial commodity of little or no lasting value. On a related note, ephemerality also creates a deep tension in the relationship between news and the truth. How can one build trust in discourse that trades on the fleetingly current? How can verifiability function in a context where the perspective is always tilted toward the emergent present? As my analysis will show, questions along these lines were a recurrent theme in public discourse around the turn of the seventeenth century. Ephemerality is central, not only to news, but also to the patterns of thinking that gradually came to govern its reception.

Narrative structure is another constitutive aspect of news—every news item tells a story. In the most minimal sense of the term, a "narrative" is a formulation that combines an agent with an action: "Santiago surrendered," "Krakatoa is erupting," and so on. On a more general level, a narrative is a complex series of agent-action combinations organized within a unifying representational framework that establishes an inherent chronological order. The representational dimension of news is easy to lose sight of because reports on current events are typically presented as a transparent window on the world, untainted by any sort of mitigation. In fact, the process of news making is actually much more creative and proactive: it links select slices of perceived reality together and arranges them into a distinctive, readily transmissible pattern—a narrative. As Hartley points out, there is an important but often slippery difference between the report of an event and the event itself: "News . . . is a discourse made into a meaningful story."[18] To draw the narratological significance of this difference into focus, think of the distinction between "event" and "news" as analogous to the distinction made by the Russian formalists between *fabula* (the elemental materials of a story) and *syuzhet* (the concrete representation used to convey the story). Contrary to what its rhetorical posture might suggest, news is not merely raw material (*fabula*) that passes through a medium without changing. Rather, it is a deliberately confected representation (*syuzhet*), a perspective on events that imposes a narrative structure. To recognize the narrative structure of news is to understand that, like any other story, news is a made thing. I want to put special emphasis on this point because my analysis focuses on how ideas develop as discourse moves into other sorts of made things, such as theater. Narrativity is particularly germane to the type of movement I analyze because it makes discourse more amenable to intermedial transfer. For example, the Duke of Buckingham's heroic account of Prince Charles's trip to Spain (1624) maintained a fundamental coherence, despite significant changes, as it moved from a speech at court, to manuscript newsletters, to polemical tracts, to Middleton's *A Game at Chess*, pulling an evolving set of ideas and attitudes along behind it. Rapid, large-scale dispersals such as these are possible primarily because of the cogency and durability of narrative structure.

As noted above, the essential difference between news narratives and theatrical narratives comes down to truthfulness. All news, including false news, posits a notional truth. By the same token, recognizing discourse as "news" necessarily involves acknowledgment of a *truth claim*, a bid for belief. For example, think of the attitude you typically adopt as you glance over the lead story on the cover of your local newspaper. You may not necessarily credit the veracity of what you read, you may not even believe in the possibility of objective truth, but by recognizing the story as news, you acknowledge that it is soliciting belief: you know that it is *pretending* to be true at the very least. This straightforward relation to the truth is common to the wide variety of texts that fall under the banner of nonfiction: history, technical manuals, menus, street signs, and so on. News is a special case, however, because its subject matter and ephemeral nature tend to generate a far higher level of skepticism and uncertainty. Nobody harbors serious general doubts about street signage: the form has a high degree of stability and very little in the way of ulterior motive, and is therefore more or less above suspicion. News on the other hand comes and goes much more quickly, thereby limiting the potential for verification, which in turn limits trustworthiness. In addition, news carries a great deal of social potency, which makes it a more likely subject of manipulation. In order to get around these problems, the idea of news had to develop a method of compensation that had an immediate impact, a way of making a truth claim compelling despite the burden of doubt brought to bear by the ephemerality and questionable subject matter necessary to the form. The eventual solution to this problem involved an authoritative, objective-sounding mode of address: a style for signifying truth. I will have more to say about this important aspect of news in the following sections, but for now it will suffice to point out that, in order to make a truth claim persuasive, one must attend to the *rhetoric* of truth. The notional truthfulness undergirding the idea of news involves a normative aesthetic, an ideal of how truth looks and sounds.

This brings me to the final part of my definition: the relation between news and a continuous, public present. I have already touched on this idea in the preceding paragraphs, but it deserves some further development because, more than any of the other features I have discussed thus far, the emergence of a public present, or at least the popular *idea* of a public present, was the ultimate precondition for the modern conception of news. As Daniel Woolf points out in a recent essay, the identification of news with the present began with a gradual recognition of a categorical difference between current events and history: "The corantos and early newsbooks of the 1620s speak of news as history and often were published under the rubric of history, a further reinforcement of the argument that at its earliest stage the published news was perceived as a record of the recent past, not of an ongoing present."[19] In Woolf's view, the conceptual disassociation of news from history marks one of the most significant accomplishments of seventeenth-century news culture: the creation of a meaningful present, a space that collapsed the temporal divide between the subjects of news and the events it described. "News had not, of course, displaced history as a subject of discussion. But it had definitively established the present as a zone of activity, as inimitable as the past, but distinguishable from it, and thereby constructed a public, space within which events could enjoy their ephemeral life before slipping into the maw of history."[20] The creation of a public present gave news a semblance of continuous actuality, a sense in the culture that it was always out there, not bracketed away from everyday experience like history, but flowing along in synch with everyday private lives. In other words, news took on the aspect of a never-ending continuum, a grand, ongoing conversation among an untold number of otherwise disconnected strangers. The popular acceptance of the notion that such a conversation could even exist, and that one could gain access to it through discourse crafted according to a particular style and structure, marks the beginning of the modern idea of news.

The Proto-Public Sphere

The body of theory underlying much of what I have said about publicity and news originates with the German sociologist and philosopher Jürgen Habermas, founder of public sphere theory. In *The Structural Transformation of the Public Sphere* (1962), Habermas sets out to explain how economic and cultural developments leading up to the eighteenth century gave rise to the "public sphere," a discursive space where individuals can come together to engage in rational-critical debate. I owe Habermas a significant debt, but I have serious disagreements with him as well, particularly in regard to the emphasis he puts on rational discourse. This section will endeavor to make my adaptation of his ideas clear, beginning with a brief summary of his core argument. For the most part, my summary will focus on the first half of *Structural Transformation*, wherein Habermas explains how public authority became the basis for liberal democracy. To put this argument in its proper context, it is important to note that the book is a response, of sorts, to theory from the Frankfurt school that framed popular media as an instrument of ideological control and a constraint on genuine freedom.[21] In contrast to this view, Habermas insists on the democratic potential of popular media, an argument he develops by showing how new forms of publicity—especially novels and newspapers—worked in conjunction with changing relations between capitalism and the state to democratize the public sphere. He begins with the observation that public representation was originally an exclusive power of courtly elites, which meant that the validity of any given assertion in public discourse hinged on personal status, not reason or popular consensus. In the eighteenth century, however, a radically different notion of publicity began to take hold. Significant social changes such as the emergence of capitalism and a middle class coincided with an enhanced focus on the private, domestic sphere, a dimension of life that gradually assumed public characteristics of its own. Literature helped to move this process along by enriching the profile and meaningfulness of privacy (as in Richardson's *Clarissa,* for example), and also by providing private people with a training ground where they could exercise their critical faculties. Empowered by a growing sense of their own social significance, private individuals gathered in forums such as coffeehouses and salons to create an incipient public sphere, a discursive space where the validity of an argument depended on reason (in principle at least), not social status.

These developments coincided with the emergence of a new conception of governmental authority. The state became an identifiable social entity, subject to public criticism from private persons who now understood themselves, not as the mere subjects of authority, but as the legitimizing force behind it: "the people." In Habermas's view, this counterpositioning of state and society helped to solidify a public sphere that implicitly encouraged the collective exercise of reason and critical judgment on matters previously open to state and religious authorities exclusively: "Because, on the one hand, the society now confronting the state clearly separated a private domain from public authority, and because, on the other hand, it turned the reproduction of life into something transcending the confines of private domestic authority and becoming a subject of public interest, that zone of continuous administrative contact became 'critical' also in the sense that it provoked the critical judgment of a public making use of its reason."[22] Literature played an important role in fostering this critical capability because it presented the public with a projected image of itself, thereby instilling "the people" with a distinct sense of identity and capability. Newspapers, in particular, began to assert the public's right to judge state affairs, explicitly marketing themselves as a forum where rational-critical debate and contests for state power could play out in public view. This emphasis on the role of reason and rational-critical discourse also underpins Habermas's argument in the second part of *Structural Transformation*, wherein he holds up the eighteenth-century public sphere as a normative ideal and contrasts it with the degenerated state of public discourse in the twentieth century. In his view, twentieth-century forms such as advertising and public relations actively derail the rational-critical debate that popular media used to promote. Ultimately, however, *Structural Transformation* holds out an optimistic hope in the progressive potential of formal democracy—the proposed antidote to the failures Habermas finds in mass culture.

Public sphere theory has evolved substantially since Habermas's pioneering work in the early 1960s. In contrast to the model of a unitary, rational-critical public sphere presented in *Structural Transformation*, many theorists now subscribe to a notion of a public sphere comprised of multiple, overlapping publics, with each public organized around an individual focus of common interest—an interest that may or may not bear a relation to rational-critical debate. As Michael Warner noted in an interview for the CBC series *Origins of the Modern Public*, although exercising reason is certainly one of the many things people do in a public, "it is very far from being the only thing that they do, and it's not even clear that it's even the most important thing."[23] To correct for Habermas's overemphasis on the role of rationality, the "plurality of publics" model posits a decentralized structure where mere discourse, rather than rational debate, functions as the connective tissue holding a public together. In an explanation of this model, Craig Calhoun describes the public sphere as a "field of discursive connections" and "publics" as "clusters of relatively greater density of communication within the looser overall field."[24] These clusters of communication "may be only more or less biased microcosms of the whole, as cities have their own public discourse within countries, and as neighborhoods within cities. But clusters may also be organized around issues, categories, persons, or basic dynamics of the larger society."[25] Following Habermas, the plurality-of-publics model posits communication as the fundamental constitutive element of the public sphere, but allows for a much broader account of how public making works: when adherents turn their attention to *any* form of discourse that takes a nonexclusive, open-ended rhetorical stance, they enter into a tacit union with each other by imagining themselves as part of a postulated public, the group of "everyone and anyone" presumptively addressed. This group is *actual* insofar as constituents actually exist in the real world, but it is also *virtual* because it derives from and depends on sustained engagement with notional constituents (the *idea* of a public). When one reads a novel, for example, one imagines, quite correctly, that there are other readers out there somewhere with whom one shares a set of common feelings and experiences. This capacity to anchor and characterize a sense of collectivity among strangers pertains to all public-oriented forms: novels, plays, paintings, music, even maps—anything confected to attract attention.

By influencing the way people conceptualize their identities and relations to others, public making exerts a very real, though indirect, influence on the social infrastructure. For example, consider the remarkable power of music to assemble publics that cut across boundaries of language, race, family, nationality, location, and so on. Even though a given body of music may not have any particular political significance in and of itself, the social entity it creates can have a transformative impact on the ground where politics play out. By changing the ways people connect to each other, public making changes the political landscape—and by changing the political landscape, it exerts an influence on the sorts of discourses and actions that count as political. This model, which we might call the "indirect theory of publics and political change," represents a marked departure from Habermas's model, where a unitary public sphere spurs political change in a more-or-less direct manner by fostering discussion in regard to political matters. Because it shifts emphasis from the *style* of public discourse to the *impact* of the social entities that public discourse creates, the "indirect" model allows for a theory of publicity that takes a fuller range of public-making activities into consideration, thereby enabling a significant expansion of Habermas's account of how news contributed to the transformation of the public sphere. Thus, in addition to noting, with Habermas, that newspapers facilitated political change by providing a forum that subjected politics to the scrutiny of public judgment, my analysis also considers extra-intellectual aspects that helped to bring that forum together. By "extra-intellectual," I mean the great variety of appeals that fall outside the narrow boundaries of rational discourse. From the very beginning, the public created by news entailed a powerful affective dimension: it enabled people to think and judge together, as Habermas notes, but also enabled them to *feel* together, to experience current events on a collective, emotional basis. With this observation in mind, I have endeavored to develop a reevaluation of the relation between news and publics that considers the ability to enrage, annoy, entertain, frighten, titillate, amuse, console, and surprise on an equal footing with the ability to foster rational judgment.

My understanding of the indirect influence that public making can have on social change derives in large part from research undertaken by the Making Publics (MaPs) project, a five-year interdisciplinary initiative that brought together a group of Canadian and American scholars under the direction of Paul Yachnin at McGill University. Following recent work on the history of publicity, MaPs researchers argued that, although a full-blown Habermasian public sphere did not exist in early modernity, the period did involve a notable proliferation of publics and public-making activity. This expansion of opportunities for participation in public life initiated a shift toward modern norms of publicity and therefore constitutes a formative stage in the emergence of the modern notion of a public sphere. Rather than a fluid field of discursive connections, the early modern proto-public sphere entailed a dispersion of discrete but intermittently connected spaces for public discourse, spaces that allowed people "to connect with others in ways not rooted in family, rank or vocation, but rather in voluntary groupings built on shared interests, tastes, commitments, and desires of individuals."[26] Although not necessarily oriented toward politics, these new forms of association "in effect challenged dominant ideas about who could be a public person, expanded resources of public life for ordinary people, and developed ideas and practices that have helped to create the political culture of modernity"[27] In the remaining section of this chapter, I will develop further examples of how this view of public making in early modernity applies to the public created by printed news.

Before that, however, a brief recap: the overarching contention of the present study is that theater played a formative role in the development of the idea of news, a literary innovation of significant political import, but not necessarily the result of any specific political motivation or intention. To develop this argument, the foregoing historical and theoretical discussion has endeavored to bring the close, complex relationship between theatrical culture and news culture into focus. I describe the relationship between the two cultures as "complex" because it operated at the level of content, but also at the level of social structure. For example, at the level of content, narratives, images, and ideas (including the idea of news) moved back and forth between drama, ballads, manuscript newsletters, printed news pamphlets, and so on, developing dialogically as a result of circulation across a variety of platforms. Moreover, at the level of social structure, the concentrations of discursive activity—or publics—galvanized by these various cultural forms exerted a pull on the evolving shape of society by radically reorganizing the way people connected to and thought about each other. To better understand this model, think of the relation between publics and early modern society as a handful of metal rings scattered across a sheet pulled tight over a frame. The rings vary in size. Three of the biggest ones are the public created by the commercial theater, the public created by commercial print, and the public created by news. They also overlap: the audience for commercial print includes many of the same people who make up the audience for commercial theater, which in turn includes many of the same people who make up the audience for news. There are also a number of smaller rings overlapping or entirely contained by the big three. For example, the public for corantos is wholly inside the public for commercial print, while the public for printed playtexts overlaps significantly, but not entirely, with the public for commercial theater. Overlap is conducive to the transfer of discourse between publics, and by the same token, transfer of discourse between publics tends to increase overlap. To understand how this discursive activity exerts a pull on the structural dimension of society, think of the publics as droplets of water, rather than metal rings. The precise configuration of the droplets is not static, but constantly changing over time: some droplets disappear, but even more droplets pop up, and for the most part, the size of droplets and overall rate of overlap increases. As this happens, the sheet begins to sag in places where the concentration of water is most dense, thereby transforming the overall field of social activity and indirectly exercising an influence on the course of political action. For the purposes of my argument, the key point in regard to this model is that a good deal of the public-making activity generating the news public overlapped significantly with public-making activity in the theatrical public and the public created by commercial print. This overlap meant that what happened in one public could have an effect on many others: discourse in the theater influenced how the news public and the print public developed, and vice versa. In order to capture a more distinct picture of how the process worked, my analysis considers the interaction of public-making practices and the idea of news across a variety of platforms, with particular focus on theater and print—partly because these two forms were uniquely potent progenitors of the idea of news, and also because, unlike other forms of discourse (such as oral conversation) they have left a record that lends itself to close study.

Public Making and Printed News

By tracing how the idea of news developed in conjunction with public-making practices in printed news pamphlets, this section endeavors to articulate key issues that will also figure prominently in my analysis of news and drama. Once again, the ultimate intention here is to show how news evolved as the result of the close, complex relationship between theater and other forums for public discourse that grappled with the same ideas, fostered the same conversations, and addressed (more or less) the same popular audience. With this goal in mind, I have selected some representative examples of printed news that capture various aspects of a public-making process in action. Most of these examples are from the early 1620s, the period when news started to become a fully-fledged industry. However, in order to develop a sense of historical perspective, I am going to begin with something much older: the earliest surviving printed pamphlet that uses the word "news" in connection to current events, *Heuy Newes of an Horryble Earth Quake whiche was in the Cytie of Scharbaria in this Present Yeare of XLII. The XIII. Day of June. Also how that a Cytie in Turky is Sonke* (1542). As its title suggests, the principal subject of this document is the severe earthquake of 1542 that all but leveled the city of Scarperia, Italy (25 km northwest of Florence). Significantly, rather than identifying a precise date of publication, the title page establishes a time frame in a roundabout, ambiguous manner by describing the year of the earthquake as "this present year," a marker that puts the production of the pamphlet within six months, at most, of the events it describes. As we will see, this passive attitude toward periodicity marks a notable difference between early news publications and the reports of the following century, which took far greater care to stake out a position that was as close as possible to an ongoing public present. In 1542, information from remote locations circulated in a temporality marked out in months and years, rather than days and weeks, so a report appearing from a distance of an indeterminate number of months could still count, quite naturally, as current. On a similar note, the long shelf life for news also explains why the publishers do not bother to offer any date at all for the other major event recorded in the pamphlet (the sinking of a city in Turkey) aside from an editorial introduction that describes the report as a "new tydynge."[28] No other markers of newness or currency are necessary because, in the mid-sixteenth century, periodicity and ephemerality had yet to become salient factors of news value. Dislocated from the regular rhythm of everyday life, the two narratives on offer in *Heuy Newes* appear as discrete, remote reports, rather than updates in a continuous, constantly changing stream of information. "News" in this context simply means "a new report"—not an interactive, ongoing public conversation.

Nevertheless, there are other areas in the document where one can see pressures central to the modern idea of news exerting an influence. The most notable feature in this regard is the emphasis on authenticity and authority, or what we might also think of as a style for signifying truthfulness. Following a common convention that would continue for more than a century, the earthquake narrative takes the form of a letter framed by an introduction in an editorial voice: "The heuy news contayned in a letter sent out of Italy."[29] An eyewitness account in the first person follows: "Rightc douty and wel-bloued Lorde I lette you wytte the pytieful new tydynge and horri-ble earthquake, which I meselfe haue sene."[30] Significantly, although the letter does not name the author or his correspondent, it begins by addressing an unspecified "Lord." The clear implication here is that the document is a printed version of a manuscript newsletter originally intended for a person of stature—handwritten copies of such letters circulated widely among members of the upper classes and remained a dominant source of printed news for much of the seventeenth century. Regardless of whether the implied source is authentic, the framing device lends the pamphlet some proximal authenticity, a sense of truthfulness that derives from the regard typically accorded to figures of authority. In other words, the letter seems trustworthy because it connects to a man of rank, a man whose public reputation would normally suggest honor and good judgment. This invocation of authority contributes to an overall style designed to garner the sort of trust that normally grows out of personal interaction. By intentionally emphasizing a connection to nobility, the document invites readers to judge its authenticity according to the same system of social cues that they would typically rely on to judge the word of a fellow human being, effectively co-opting the logic of social interaction in order to make a truth claim in text. On a similar note, it is significant that the author stipulates, in the very first sentence, that he bore personal witness to the events described in the report. In a society where communication is predominantly oral, eyewitness testimony takes on a particular weight: one can judge the truth of a report by observing the appearance and demeanor of the reporter. In order to exploit the special credibility generally associated with eyewitness testimony, news publishers of the 1590s regularly hired professional writers to recast translations of foreign news as first-person accounts told in the voice of someone who had (purportedly) experienced the events he is recounting.[31] Although it is impossible to know if *Heuy Newes* is the product of similar refashioning, there can be little doubt that its producers deliberately adopted an overall style designed to encourage belief. As is the case with all news, the document seeks to assure readers of its legitimacy by claiming a direct, transparent relation to the truth.

The pamphlet's attempt to build trust by mimicking the dynamics of personal interaction overlaps with the other primary element of its appeal: emotional intensity. One need not look any further than the first two words emblazoned prominently across the top of the title page to understand that the reading experience on offer promises significant affective weight. As one might reasonably expect, the adjective "heavy" in the title refers, not only to the magnitude of physical destruction in Scarperia, but also to an expected (and directed) emotional impact, the feelings of horror and sympathy readers will likely experience as they acquire vivid, vicarious knowledge of what the earthquake looked and felt like to the people who experienced it firsthand. For an example of the sort of heaviness on offer, consider the following excerpt from the fourth page. Shortly after telling how the earthquake shook him awake one morning while he was sleeping in a bed at an inn, the author describes the scene of devastation that he witnessed as he rushed through the city to safety:

> But within the cytie are nearehande sonke and broken all the houses, and some folke peryshed. The churches & greate howses are all fallen to the grounde. The people that was lefte in lyfe dyd crye Misericorde with great chatte-rynge of tethe, by reason of the feare, and ranne out of the citie into a moras grounde, where we were fledde also with our ooste and his housholde. Helas for pitie, there was so pytieful an outcrye and howlynge of men and women, as I never dyd heare all the days of my lyfe.[32]

Notice the density of acute, visceral detail working to create a sense of emotional impact: the sound of teeth chattering in fear, a chorus of voices howling in pity, survivors running for their lives, and so on. At the risk of overdetermining the relevance of a solitary example, I want to suggest that this intense focus on how the victims of the earthquake felt is indicative of an affective appeal that has always been an important part of how news makes a public. As noted above, the prospective reward for the consumer of news lies, not only in gaining access to information about current events, but also in gaining a sense of closeness to public conversation, a feeling that one has gained knowledge of "what people are talking about," regardless of whatever specific details the conversation might entail. By the same token, we might also say that news value derives, in part, from the pleasure of connecting to "what people are feeling," a sense of emotional communion. Like the myriad publications that would follow its example, *Heuy Newes* capitalizes on the satisfaction of sharing an emotional experience with others, an elementary form of human comfort. By stirring feelings of empathy and horror, the pamphlet created something of substance and value that people could share, thereby introducing opportunities for public connectedness.

Ultimately, however, *Heuy Newes* offers little more than an oblique hint at a public-making process that may or may not have existed—there is very little evidence to show how it may have fit into a larger public conversation. This is less of an issue with the news publications of the 1620s, not only because there are more documents to study, but also because the extant documents demonstrate a marked concern to present themselves in relation to a notion of ongoing discursive activity. For example, the corantos of the early 1620s regularly appeared under the title "Corant or weekly newes," even though they most likely circulated on an erratic, semiregular basis.[33] This pretension toward "weekliness" had two important rhetorical effects. First, it posited the publication as a link in a chain, a text connected to a concatenation of other texts that have come before and will continue to come after.[34] Second, it enhanced a sense of closeness to a public present, to "what people are talking about this week." This concern to appear within the context of an ongoing, current conversation became increasingly prominent as the commercial news industry developed. By 1625, most publishers had adopted the convention of identifying news publications with a date and installment number at the top of the front page, a practice that has survived to the present day. On a similar note, it also became quite common for the word "continuation" to appear in titles, a motif that helped to cultivate a notion of news as an unbroken procession of discourse made manifest over a regularly updated series of installments. Such trends contributed, inevitably, to the growing connection between ephemerality and news value. For example, consider how a focus on ephemerality, currency, and periodicity come together in *The Continuation of our Newes from the 4. to the 17 of this instant*, the title of a news pamphlet published by Nathaniel Butter in 1630. In contrast to the mid-sixteenth-century conventions that characterize *Heuy Newes*, the demands of news value now obligated publishers to market their commodity, not as the product of "this year" or even "this month," but as a product of "this instant," a direct, continuous connection to the discursive network undergirding public life.

The ensemble of textual features that helped to situate news within a context of an ongoing public conversation went well beyond the new systems of numbering and dating. Most notably, the editorial preface, a well-established device adapted from other narrative forms (including drama), brought significant depth and texture to the overall impression of a lively discursive community. For example, consider the preface to *The Strangling and Death of the Great Turke* (1622), a pamphlet by the most famous news writer of the day, Captain Thomas Gainsford (the model for Jonson's "Captain" in *The Staple of News*). Imitating epic grandiosity, Gainsford begins his introduction by offering elaborate thanks to God for the recent murder of Sultan Osman II of Turkey, a key foe of the Protestant cause in the Thirty Years' War (Gainsford and his publisher, Nathaniel Butter, were keen supporters of England's Protestant allies). After a lengthy, ornate sentence describing how God had "put an hook in the nostrils of Leviathan, and kept him from devouring poore Christians,"[35] he surprises readers with a sudden shift in tone:

> Where are your dreaming Gazettes, and Coranto's now, that talkt of such formidable preparation, and so many hundred thousand in an Army? Where is the threatening of Poland, and terrifying the Cossacks with so many thousand Tartarians? Where is their coming into Hungary, to begin a new Warre there? What all husht and quiet?[36]

This series of stridently ironic questions explicitly attacks, and imitates, the reports of other corantos, a maneuver that adds acute detail to the discursive assembly projected into the background. A few pages on, the editor's object of derision appears in even greater focus:

> I can but wonder at the shamelesse reports of strange men, and weake Certificates by Corantes from Foraine parts, especially to haue them Printed, to talke of so many Thousands slaine, the Prince kill'd, Sigismond defeated, and the whole Army put to flight, when yet as I said, there was neuer any such matter, nor any set Battaile fought.[37]

With the phrase "from foreign parts" Gainsford directs his attack toward corantos deriving from Italy, a primary source of material for English news publications. This rhetorical stance is notable from a public-making perspective because, as the editor was undoubtedly aware, the chance that he might actually reach his ostensible addressees was extremely slim (there was not much of a market for English corantos outside of England). But, of course, reaching Italy was never Gainsford's objective. Like a stage general bellowing orders at an army beyond view, he indirectly communicates with his actual audience in England by projecting a virtual audience that stretches across all of Europe. The forum he implies is a dynamic, expansive space open to a great variety of opinion and actors, a space that cuts across boundaries of religion, politics, and geography. In short, it is the public space postulated by the new idea of news.

With the axiomatic relationship between news and truth in mind, it is also important to note that the occasion for Gainsford's special attention to his field of discourse involves an accusation of falsity. The Italian corantos deserve condemnation, he suggests, because they repeatedly printed reports that exaggerated or lied about the "formidable preparations" and accomplishments of the Italian and Spanish armies: "terrifying the Cossacks with so many thousand Tartarians," "coming into Hungary to begin a new war," "the Prince killed," "Sigismond defeated," and so on. This line of attack entails two positive assertions: (1) news publications ought to tell the truth, and (2) in contrast to the Italian corantos, Gainsford's news is true. On the surface, the first assertion might seem too obvious to warrant attention, but I would argue that its obviousness is partly the result of a hard-fought battle over news-truthfulness that began in earnest in the early seventeenth century and continues to this day. Normative standards, such as "news should be true," become codified in the social imaginary as a result of public jockeying among a diversity of public agents. Regardless of the contestants' intentions, a disputation over which party has the greater claim on a given property will inevitably increase agreement on the overall value of whatever happens to be at stake (in this case, truth). Thus, by pushing an accusation of falsity, Gainsford tacitly reinforces consensus around the idea that truthfulness is an important and necessary property of news, a property presumably worth fighting over and defending at great cost. The establishment of this important patch of common ground adds force and meaning to the second positive assertion in Gainsford's attack: the suggestion that, unlike the Italian corantos, his news is true. Like the first assertion, this implicit claim develops out of a context of diversity, a discursive field that allows for the possibility of multiple public agents jockeying over various other truth claims—some valid, others not. Gainsford promotes consensual standards, and signals his own conformity to those standards, by contrasting himself against a range of players jostling for attention in an active, wide-ranging news public.

Of course, the discursive jostling and posturing of the news public occurred, not only among publishers, but also among the consumers and other adherents engaged in the conversation around current events. As Michael Warner has noted, the *Spectator* made representation of these important actors a standard feature of periodicals in the eighteenth century, anticipating a wide variety of mechanisms—such as "viewer mail, call-in shows, 900-number polling, home video shows, game show contestants, town meetings, studio audiences, and man-on-the-street interviews"—that enable mass media "to characterize their own space of consumption."[38] Although such mechanisms were not a fixed feature of news publications in the early seventeenth century, incipient manifestations of the same basic pattern, or what Warner refers to as a "feedback loop," occasionally appeared in prefaces and other areas of editorial exposition.[39] For example, consider how Gainsford develops a semblance of reciprocity in the following preface to *The Affaires of Italy* (1623):

> Gentle Readers; for I am sure you would faine be knowne by that Character, how comes it then to passe, that nothing can please you? For either custome is so predominant with you, or corruption of nature carries such a mastring handl that you must be finding faults, though you know no cause. If we afford you plaine stuffe, you complaine of the phrase, and peraduenture cry out, it is Non-sense; if we adde some exornation, then are you curious to examine the method and coherence, and are forward in saying the sentences are not well adapted: if the newes bee forcible against the Emperour, you breake . . . it is impossible and is all inuention: if it tend to the deiection of the Country, you seeke to commiserate and wonder at the misfortune; if we talke of nouelty indeed, you make a doubt of the verity; if wee onely tell you what we know, you throw away the booke, and breake out, there is nothing in it, or else it is but a repetition of the former weekes newes: In a word, whateuer we endeauor is wrested by . . . passion; and whether good or bad, is fashioned to strange formes by the violence of humour, and ouerswayings of opinion. (A3v)[40]

Although this flourish of parodic ventriloquism may not achieve quite the same level of reciprocity as a "letters to the editor" section, it manages to create a more or less similar impression by staging a mock dialogue between editor and reader. Assuming a remonstrative tone, the "editorial voice" protests that, although readers have trouble making sense of unadorned translations ("plain stuff"), any effort to make the text more accessible ("exornation") leads them to suspect inaccuracy. Continuing through a list of grievances paired in a similar fashion, he adds that, while readers tend to doubt any news of a favorable nature, they always get upset when the news is bad, and although they reject "novelty" reports (strange births, miracles, etc.) as nonsense, they also grumble about stories that merely adhere to known fact. A sense of personality at the source of all these complaints comes to life with the addition of direct quotations ("it is nonsense," "the sentences are not well adapted," etc.) and a few strokes of physical detail ("you cry out," "you throw away the book"). As noted in the example from *The Strangling and Death of the Great Turke*, this vivid characterization of a field of discourse converges with a number of tensions central to the public-making practice of printed news, particularly the struggle over truthfulness. More pertinently, the passage also bears significant structural and tonal resemblances to the public-making practices of the commercial theater. Reflexive representation may have featured infrequently in early seventeenth-century news, but it was a well-established aspect of theatrical representation, and quite often assumed the same parodic, remonstrative posture exhibited in both of the editorial introductions quoted above. I will return to this pattern of representation in my discussion of Jonson's *The Staple of News* and (to a lesser extent) Middleton's *A Game at Chess*, where it will become an important pillar in my analysis of news and theatrical public making. For now, however, I would like to set out a few more thoughts about an issue that connects to almost everything I have said thus far: how the idea of news contributed to the reinvention of truth.

For the most part, our sense of the mind-set people adopted in regard to news derives from secondhand sources such as Gainsford's prefaces, but there are also a few, very rare, documents that offer a more direct representation of reader response. Consider, for example, the only surviving copy of *The Continuation of Our Weekely Newes, from the 16 August to the 24 of the Same* (1626), a Butter publication preserved in the library at Belvoir Castle, Leicestershire. In the description of this document for his *Bibliography of English Corantos and Periodical Newsbooks* (1952), Folke Dahl records a number of marginal notes in a contemporary hand, including the short comment "good yf true" next to the report of a Protestant victory. Dahl interprets the comment as an expression of doubt over the "reliability of newsbooks," which seems correct, but I would add that the doubt is of a provisional, rather than cynical, nature.[41] In other words, it suggests cautious optimism, an inclination to reserve judgment until further information becomes available: *The report is good, but only if it's true . . . let's wait and see.* This manner of engagement is significant because it reflects a way of thinking about truth conditioned by exposure to a continuous stream of divergent reports—a dynamic, heterogeneous news culture that forces subjects to develop discriminatory reading habits, to compare various reports against each other, and to think of truth, not as an absolute property, but as a nuanced, inconstant impression that evolves over time. On a more general level, it also reflects a vexed, transformative rethinking of truth that figures prominently throughout the cultural production of the period. In one way or another, all of the examples discussed thus far show this concern over truth working in conjunction with an active public-making practice, beginning with the early, stylistic attempts to suggest truthfulness in *Heuy Newes* and progressing toward the more sophisticated devices employed in Gainsford's prefaces. To conclude, I want to introduce one more example from Gainsford that captures a uniquely candid moment of truth-reinvention in action. The following is from the preface to *Late Newes or True Relations* 30 (2 July 1624):

> I thinke it not vnfit to resolue a question which was lately made vnto mee viz. wherefore I would publish any tidings which were only rumoured without any certainty: I will answer that I doe it to shew both my loue and diligence to the vnpartiall Reader. And that I rather will write true tidings only to be rumoured, when I am not fully sure of them, then to write false tidings to bee true, which will afterwards proue otherwise.[42]

Gainsford's recharacterization of rumor amounts to an editorial analogue for "good yf true." It is appropriate to print uncertain reports, he argues, because news is always subject to correction—anything he publishes is either true or "will afterwards prove otherwise" . . . just wait and see. As Marcus Nevitt has pointed out, this justification recasts rumor as a new "kind of truth," ideally "suited to serialized narrative": Gainsford minimizes objection to false reports with reassurances that they "can always be corrected at a later date," but also shifts the ultimate responsibility of judgment to the "reader's interpretive ability."[43] In short, he has asserted an epistemology that makes truth a matter one must decide for oneself, over time, in relation to a continuing stream of information—an epistemology inherent to the modern idea of news. As I will argue in the next chapter, this radically contingent, time-bound notion of truth put significant pressure on the classical ideal of truth as a transhistorical, permanent, and unchanging absolute—thereby creating a tension that is central to Shakespeare's analysis of news culture in *The Winter's Tale.*

CHAPTER 2

The Winter's Tale, News, Truth, and Belief

The Winter's Tale is an extended meditation on truth and belief: how to evaluate the truthfulness of any given reality, how to know what to believe, how to accommodate uncertainty. Thinking through these problems, Shakespeare develops a narrative that moves from unbridled skepticism (radical doubt) to faith (radical belief), passing over various manifestations of truth and nontruth, belief and nonbelief, along the way. As his investigation proceeds, he finds a particularly rich focus for reflection in the emergence of news, a form he interrogates alongside a variety of other ways of knowing and telling, including dreams, balladry, gossip, rumor, romance, oracular revelation, drama, the testimony of women, and (as the title suggests) tales. The present chapter tracks this process of interrogation with particular attention to how questions presented by news culture flow into a broader epistemological inquiry. Following a brief discussion of how news functions throughout the Shakespearean corpus, I develop a detailed explication of the historical context underlying Autolycus and the parodic reports he purveys, one of the first representations of a public, commercial news market in the period. This analysis lays the groundwork for an interpretation of the play as an early exercise in media criticism—a study of news inextricably caught up with the making of the *idea of news* itself.

Shakespeare and News

What news? (Cymbeline 1.1.161)[1]
Now what news? (2 Henry IV 2.4.354)
Sirrah, what news? (Julius Caesar 5.3.25)
What news abroad? (King John 5.6.17)
What's the news? What's the news? (Coriolanus 4.6.85)
What news? (King Lear 4.2.70)
What news, what news, in this our tottering state? (Richard III 3.2.36)

According to the Open Source Shakespeare Concordance, the word "news" occurs 317 times in 297 speeches within thirty-eight of the dramatist's works, putting it within the top 300 most frequently occurring words in a canon comprising 28,829 individual word forms (words occurring at a roughly similar rate include, "lie," "things," "fortune," "fellow," "help," "hands," and "bed").[2] Distribution patterns suggest the frequency of the word may depend, to a limited extent, on genre: all of the plays in which it appears most often are histories and tragedies (twenty-seven occurrences in *2 Henry IV* and *Richard III*, twenty in *Coriolanus*, seventeen in *3 Henry VI*, sixteen in *King John*, thirteen in *Antony and Cleopatra*, twelve in *Romeo and Juliet* and *1 Henry IV*), but it also appears with notable frequency in a few comedies (twelve occurrences in *The Merchant of Venice*, eleven in *Two Gentlemen of Verona*). Notably, in a little more than a third of all instances where it appears, the word is part of a variation on "What news?" ("What is the news?"), a question that Shakespearean characters ask approximately 120 times, usually in connection to battles or affairs of state, but also in less elevated, domestic contexts, such as a wedding feast (*Taming of the Shrew* 5.2.83), or a private conversation in an orchard (*Romeo and Juliet* 2.5.18). In a number of cases, the question cues exposition from a messenger or other sort of reporter who narrates events that Shakespeare could not or did not want to represent onstage—for example, the Boatswain reports the miraculous restoration of Alonso's ship when Gonzalo asks for news in *The Tempest* (5.1.221–24), and the Second Messenger reports the death of Fulvia when Antony asks for news in *Antony and Cleopatra* (1.2.119–24). Dramatic utility aside, the frequency of "What news?" is also explainable as a straightforward reflection of contemporary speech. As Atherton has noted, the question was a standard salutation in the sixteenth and seventeenth centuries, the form of address an early modern would typically adopt when encountering a person who had just arrived from a remote locale (a person such as a traveling player, perhaps, or an itinerant peddler on the model of

Autolycus).[3] Considering the centrality of the theater to public life in early modern London, one can reasonably presume that the question was also frequently on the lips and minds of Shakespeare's audience members as they filed in and out of the Globe. The appeal of news was a powerful aspect of the drama proper, but it was also an important part of being physically present in and around the theater, one of the very few venues where large groups could congregate voluntarily around a mutual interest.

Of course, the subject of the present study is not simply the word "news" itself, but the new idea of news that evolved in conjunction with new media products, increased mechanisms for transmitting information, and increased opportunities for participation in public life. Shakespeare's career in the theater falls somewhere around the middle phase of this process of evolution, beginning about the same time that John Wolfe published his short-lived series of news quartos on the French wars in the early 1590s, overlapping with the increased availability and popularity of news that characterized the first decade of the seventeenth century, and ending in 1613, seven years before Nathaniel Butter and his partners would form the nation's first news syndicate and begin to produce regular installments of news serials on a weekly basis. This chronology is important to keep in mind because it foregrounds the significance that a difference of a decade can potentially bring to bear on what "news culture" might mean in an early modern context. News was in a state of intense flux on a conceptual, technological, and social level in the years around the turn of the seventeenth century. The media landscape Shakespeare surveyed when he wrote *The Winter's Tale* in 1609–10 looked appreciably different when Ben Jonson took up the same subject for *The Staple of News* in 1626 (a contrast comparable, in a very general sense, to the contrast between the television cultures of 1948 and 1964, or the Internet cultures of 1996 and 2012). The primary task at hand in the present analysis, therefore, is not so much a matter of tracking instances in drama where news (or "news") appears, but of asking how news-thinking and the representation of news in drama contributed to an ongoing process of conceptual construction—how Shakespeare opened up a forum where people could think through the meanings of news on a critical, but also an emotional, basis.

So, what patterns appear when Shakespearean characters ask about, react to, reflect on, and report news? Turning once again to the Shakespeare Concordance, one immediately notices an emphasis on the negative. Characters describe news as "bad" (*Antony and Cleopatra*

1.2.101), "unwelcome" (*1 Henry IV* 1.1.50), "heavy" (*All's Well That Ends Well* 3.2.33), "fearful" (*Coriolanus* 4.6.145), "villainous," (*1 Henry IV* 2.4.330), "cold" (*2 Henry VI* 1.1.235), "baleful" (*3 Henry VI* 2.1.96), "full of grief" (*3 Henry VI* 4.4.13), "unsavoury" (*2 Henry VI* 4.6.80), "ill" (*King John* 4.2.134), "dead" (*King John* 5.7.65), "strange" (*Antony and Cleopatra* 3.5.2), "foul shrewd" (*King John* 5.5.14), and most forcefully of all, "black, fearful, comfortless, and horrible" (*King John* 5.6.22). Conversely, there are only four, comparatively prosaic, descriptors that cast news in a positive light: "good" (*Antony and Cleopatra* 1.3.19), "welcome" (*1 Henry IV* 1.1.66), "excellent" (*Coriolanus* 1.3.90), and "happy" (2 *Henry IV* 4.4.109).[4] On this note, I should add that in cases where good news appears, it is often a deceptive reverse-image of bad news yet to come, a pattern that recurs in *Antony and Cleopatra, Coriolanus, Macbeth, 2 Henry IV,* and *King John.* More importantly, there is also a pattern of association between the predominantly unpleasant quality of news and the unpleasant, ravenous individuals caught up in the process of transmission. For example, Lear speaks of the "poor rogues" who "talk of court news" in prison (*King Lear* 5.3.13–14), and Prince Hal says that the court itself is beleaguered by "smiling pickthanks and base newsmongers" (*1 Henry IV* 3.2.25). On a similar note, the disguised Duke in *Measure for Measure* says that there is "a great fever on goodness . . . novelty is only in request" when Escalus asks him for news (3.2.218–19), and Hamlet jokes that "doomsday" must be imminent if, as Rosencrantz claims, the only news from abroad is that "the world's grown honest" (*Hamlet* 2.2.236–38).

All of these examples reflect an abiding interest in problems concomitant to the onset of new forms of publicity. Shakespeare repeatedly emphasizes the lurid, common character of news culture, allowing for very little distance between news and rampant rumor. A particularly evocative example occurs in *King John* 4.2, where Hubert de Burgh describes the street-level conversation surrounding the (supposed) death of Arthur and an impending invasion by the French army:

> Old men and beldams in the streets
> Do prophesy upon it dangerously.
> Young Arthur's death is common in their mouths,
> And, when they talk of him, they shake their heads
> And whisper one another in the ear;
> And he that speaks doth grip the hearer's wrist,
> Whilst he that hears makes fearful action,

With wrinkled brows, with nods, with rolling eyes.
I saw a smith stand with his hammer, thus,
The whilst his iron did on the anvil cool,
With open mouth swallowing a tailor's news;
Who, with his shears and measure in his hand,
Standing on slippers, which his nimble haste
Had falsely thrust upon contrary feet,
Told of a many thousand warlike French
That were embattlèd and ranked in Kent:
Another lean unwashed artificer
Cuts off his tale and talks of Arthur's death.

(4.2.186–203)

There is something subtly grotesque in the abundance of corporeal imagery layered onto this description. The "common" news travels from mouth to mouth like a disease. People whisper in each other's ears. An animated listener nods his head and rolls his eyes, clownishly excited by the thrilling horror of the revelation. In addition to this unsettling cluster of somatic detail, there is also a prominent focus on the low social status of the individuals participating in the scene of transmission: a tailor and a blacksmith discuss the prospect of a French invasion as they go about their labors, conspicuously armed with the emblematic tools of their respective professions (hammer, anvil, shears, measure). In the midst of their exchange, the tailor is interrupted by a third craftsmen whom De Burgh refers to as "*another* lean, unwashed artificer," a description that sweepingly characterizes all parties to the conversation as filthy and underfed—and by implication, uneducated, unintelligent, and unfit to discuss matters that should properly remain within the exclusive purview of the aristocracy. As a complement to the overall tone of disparagement and mistrust, the term "artificer," or "skilled worker," also hints at spurious embellishment, just as the description of the tailor's report as a "tale" suggests an obviously fictional, baseless flight of fancy.

This vivid portrait of oral transmission readily recalls the induction to *2 Henry IV,* memorably delivered by Rumor, a stock allegorical figure popularly associated with the indiscriminate circulation of information that may or may not be true.[5] Adorned in a costume "painted full of tongues" (Induction 1), Rumor begins the play with a vision of news culture that transposes the domestic network of ears and mouths in *King John* to a global context:[6]

Open your ears, for which of you will stop
The vent of hearing when loud Rumor speaks?
I, from the orient to the drooping west,
Making the wind my post-horse, still unfold
The acts commencèd on this ball of earth.
Upon my tongues continual slanders ride,
The which in every language I pronounce,
Stuffing the ears of men with false reports.
I speak of peace while covert enmity,
Under the smile of safety, wounds the world.
And who but Rumor, who but only I,
Make fearful musters and prepared defense,
Whiles the big year, swol'n with some other grief,
Is thought with child by the stern tyrant War,
And no such matter? Rumor is a pipe
Blown by surmises, jealousies, conjectures,
And of so easy and so plain a stop
That the blunt monster with uncounted heads,
The still-discordant wav'ring multitude,
Can play upon it. But what need I thus
My well-known body to anatomize
Among my household?

(Induction 1–22)

Although the immediate focus is on orality, there are a number of details to suggest that the scene of transmission described in this extraordinary passage is in fact a depiction of the more sophisticated and diverse news culture that developed around the turn of the century.[7] In contrast to traditional mechanisms for circulating information, Rumor's network extends across the entire world ("ball of earth") and has the capacity to swiftly transmit "continual" reports, unbounded by barriers of language or geography. From this point of view, the reference to "the Orient" in line 3 takes on particular significance: one of the most prominent focuses of international news in the late sixteenth century was the Ottoman Empire, which defeated a combined Hapsburg-Transylvanian alliance in 1596, the year before *2 Henry IV* appeared at the Globe (another, much more overt allusion to the Ottomans occurs at 5.2.48, when the Prince anachronistically refers to the succession of the notorious sultan Mehmed III Adli: "This is the English, not the Turkish court; / Not Amurath an Amurath succeeds, / But Harry Harry!"). More notably, Rumor's network also entails a nonexclusive, open-ended constituency, or "wavering multitude," an assembly that sounds very much like the idea of a public posited at the foundation of the new idea of news. Following a scathing excoriation that ends with a description of his network as a "blunt monster with uncounted heads," Rumor turns to the audience assembled at the Globe and says, in effect, "you realize of course that the monster I'm talking about is *you*": "But what need I thus / My well-known body to anatomize / Among my household?" This sudden about-face opens up a more complex, more ambivalent, perspective on the public dissemination of news. Shakespeare has a sharp sense of the vulgarity and mendacity characterizing public discourse, but he also recognizes that his own profession bears an inextricable connection to it. The theater is Rumor's "household," a uniquely public forum where a messy, often unsavory, exchange of information and ideas could flourish.

Rumor's induction sets up a scene that rehearses another important pattern in Shakespeare's representation of news: the dramatization of an individual in crisis subjected to a flurry of contradictory reports. The individual in this particular case is the Earl of Northumberland, who begins the play in a state of extreme anxiety as he waits for information about his son, Henry Percy (or Hotspur), leader of the rebel army that faced off against the King's forces in the final scene of *1 Henry IV*. His first messenger, Lord Bardolph, brings purportedly "certain news" (1.1.12) of a rebel victory, a report that becomes immersed in doubt following the entry of another messenger, Travers, who says that he has just heard from a man on a bloody horse that the "rebellion had bad luck, / And that young Harry Percy's spur was cold" (1.1.41–42). As Northumberland struggles to sort out the truth of the situation, a third messenger, Morton, arrives with eyewitness testimony of the rebels' defeat and Hotspur's death, a report the Earl reluctantly accepts. Shifting, almost automatically, from news recipient to news broadcaster, he orders the immediate dispatch of "posts and letters" to circulate word of a renewed rebellion, thereby providing new grist for Rumor's myriad-headed monster to feed on (1.1.214). As noted above, the scene reprises a dramatic situation that repeatedly becomes manifest in Shakespeare's plays when serious thinking about the news occurs: an anxious, bewildered enquirer struggles to find meaning in a hazy profusion of information. For another example, consider the beginning of *Othello* 1.3, wherein the Duke of Venice, inundated by a series of wildly divergent reports, declares in frustration that "There is no composition in these news / That gives them credit" (1.3.1–2). The same pattern also appears, with particular frequency, in *Antony and Cleopatra*, a play that, as Janet Adelman has noted, continually bombards the audience "with messengers of one kind or another, not so much to convey information as to convey the sense that all information is unreliable, that it is message or rumor, not fact."[8] As noted in the foregoing analysis of Rumor's speech, Adelman finds that the pattern points back toward the speaking situation of the theater itself, reminding the audience of their complicity in the jumble of discursive activity represented onstage: "our opaque protagonists [are] surrounded by critics and commentators," she writes; "the structure of these scenes emphasizes the process of discussion."[9] Taking the argument a step further, she very helpfully points out that the dramaturgical purpose of such moments is not to condemn or confound the audience, but to prompt a more active thinking-through of the issues offered for consideration:

> We listen to a series of reports and judgments which are neither true nor false, or are both together, until even the concepts of truth and falsity lose their meanings. Shakespeare is not dallying with us only to confuse us. He is instead deliberately playing with these dramatic techniques in order to draw us into the act of judging. In effect, we are forced to judge and shown the folly of judging at the same time: our double responses are an essential part of the play.[10]

This argument returns focus to my primary object of study: the relationship between the early modern theater and what I have called "news thinking," or the conceptual construction work that laid the foundation for a new, more sophisticated, idea of news. The disorienting effect of news as it appears in Shakespeare's plays does not merely extend or reflect the disorientation of news consumers in early modernity—it transfers the experience to a wholly different register, a forum where they could think through their feelings about the news from a more critical, comfortably detached, angle of view.

Autolycus, Broadsheets, and Mercury

Autolycus does not appear in *The Winter's Tale* until the third scene of the fourth act, shortly after the action has shifted from Sicilia to Bohemia. In sharp contrast to the grave subject matter dominating the first half of the play (royal tirades, a trial, etc.), he enters singing a lighthearted song in celebration of the wayfaring life and associated pleasures such as birdsong, "ale," and "tumbling in the hay" with casual lovers (4.3.1–22). When his song comes to an end, he delivers a candid self-introduction in the style of Vice figures from Tudor morality plays, thereby establishing a confederacy with the audience and exposing his close connection to petty crime, mendacity, vagabondism, illicit sex, the placeless market, and—most significantly for the present analysis—news:

> My traffic is sheets—when the kite builds, look to lesser linen. My father named me Autolycus, who being, as I am, littered under Mercury, was likewise a snapper-up of unconsidered trifles. With die and drab I purchased this caparison, and my revenue is the silly cheat. Gallows and knock are too powerful on the highway. Beating and hanging are terrors to me. For the life to come, I sleep out the thought of it. (4.3.23–30)

Although he was once in the service of Prince Florizel (according to his own dubious claim),[11] Autolycus now makes his living by pulling "silly cheats" and by stealing "unconsidered trifles" such as bed sheets hung out to dry. In a prodigal-style confession unburdened by shame or regret, he cheerily informs the audience that he has ruined himself by gambling and whoring ("die and drab"), and must therefore go about in tattered rags, attire he refers to with ironic floridity as "this caparison" (fashionable garb). Admitting a wariness of occupational hazards such as "beating and hanging," he also notes his tendency to use obscure roads away from the "highway," a style of travel that enables him to move from town to town without fear of the authorities—or for that matter, God himself ("the life to come"). As was the case with the celebrated occultist and playgoer Simon Forman, most spectators at the Globe would have immediately recognized in this shameless, flyblown character an iteration of the "masterless man": an itinerant, rootless figure belonging to the shadowy margins of society and known for his ability to live by his wits rather than manual labor.[12] Such men—wandering peddlers, balladeers, pimps, pickpockets, cheats of various stripes—became a familiar fixture in London toward the end of the sixteenth century, the product of rapid urban expansion and the shift to a more fluid economic order based on cash and credit rather than land and title. Celebrated in print and on stage by the "cony-catching" pamphlets and witty city comedies of Greene, Middleton, and Jonson, they attracted admiration for their good humor and romantic (or romanticized) lifestyle, but were also a source of significant anxiety: people saw them as a threat, not only to unsuspecting individual victims, but to social discipline in general.[13]

In the character of Autolycus, Shakespeare develops a pattern of association—already present in the culture to a certain extent—that conflates the seaminess of masterless men with the seaminess of news, a process that begins with the clever tri-valency in the first sentence of the introduction: "My traffic is sheets" (4.3.23). As noted, "sheets" refers, first of all, to bed sheets, a typical target for petty thieves. In addition, it also refers to sex, or—when combined with "traffic"—to pimping, a meaning that becomes especially available when placed in the mouth of a shady character such as Autolycus. Mingling among the connections to thieving and whoring, there is also a reference to "broadsheets," large sections of inexpensive paper used to print the broadside ballads sold by peddlers and balladeers. I will have much more to say about these documents in the following paragraphs, but for the moment it will suffice to point out, as a placeholder, that they played an important role in framing how people of the period thought about the developing phenomenon of news (a function also served by the theater, as I have been arguing). On a similar note, the second sentence of the introduction drops a quick reference to the rogue's Ovidian namesake, thereby deploying a second, richly multivalent association between news and dishonesty. As Shakespeare is eager to remind his audience, the mythological Autolycus was the son of Mercury, the god responsible for transmitting information, but also (paradoxically) the god of thieving and lying, traits that Ovid also attributes to the son: "he could make white black and black white, a worthy heir of his father's art."[14] The Ovidian Autolycus and the Shakespearean Autolycus were both "littered [born] under Mercury," as Autolycus notes, because the former was the actual son of the god, and the latter was born while Mercury (the planet) was in ascendancy. There is also a clear affinity in terms of character: like his Ovidian namesake, the Shakespearean Autolycus is a "snapper-up of unconsidered trifles," a petty thief and liar warranting maximum suspicion. In addition to these resonances, the prominently declared connection to Mercury posits a second allusion to news: the *Mercurius Gallobelgicus* was Europe's first branded periodical, a weighty, semiannual compendium of news in Latin, specializing in military reports from France and the Low Countries.[15] Each issue featured an image of Mercury—bringer of information—on the cover. Taken together, Autolycus's references to (broad)sheets and Mercury amount to a subtle, but clear, indication of a focus on news culture. Shakespeare presents an unscrupulous, vagabond salesman associated with various aspects of commercial print—an avatar, in effect, of news as it appeared on the streets of London around 1611.

A closer look at the historical context of printed news will help to bring the cultural resonance of "Mercury" into greater relief. As noted, one of the key referents for this signifier is *Mercurius Gallobelgicus,* a Latin compendium that originated in Italy in 1594, made its way to England soon thereafter, and became available in English translation somewhere around 1603.[16] One of the publication's many legacies is that it made the word "Mercury" synonymous with the purveyors of news and news in general, an import that persisted into the nineteenth century (*OED*). As noted above, however, the name also carried a mischievous, unintended resonance for anyone familiar with mythology: in addition to his role as a bringer of information, Mercury was the god of theft and lying. Shakespeare was not the first poet to exploit this extra layer of meaning for satirical purposes. For example, consider John Donne's epigram *Mercurius Gallobelgicus* (most likely written somewhere between 1598 and 1608):[17]

> Like Æsops fellowe slaves, (O Mercury!)
> Which could doe allthings, thy fayth is, and I,
> Like Æsops selfe, which nothing: I confesse
> I should have had more fayth, if thou hadst lesse
> Thy credit lost thy credit; 'tis sinne to doe
> In this case as thou wouldst be done unto,
> To beleive all: chaunge thy name, thou arte like
> Mercury in stealing, and ly'st like a Greeke.[18]

Donne begins with an allusion to Aesop[19] that mocks *Mercurius* for its putatively omniscient worldview (or knowledge of "all things"), an implicit accusation of fraudulence that he extends in the succeeding lines with a direct accusation of credulity: "thy credit lost thy credit" (your willingness to believe everything makes it impossible for readers to believe anything you say). Suggesting that such qualities warrant an exception to the golden rule, he adds that he cannot invest in *Mercurius* the same level of belief that he would normally desire for himself because it would be a sin to "to believe all," as *Mercurius* requires ("'tis sinne to doe / In this case as thou wouldst be done unto"). As Smith notes, this witty formulation leads to an analogy between the mythological Mercury's reputation for theft and *Mercurius*'s reputation for "filching scraps of news from all quarters without acknowledgement," a comparison one might also infer from Autolycus's self-description as a "snapper-up of unconsidered trifles."[20] More generally, the epigram also points to the same basic tensions in news culture that Shakespeare grapples with in *The Winter's Tale*. As is the case with Donne, the dramatist views news as the product of symbiotic impulses: unlimited credulity on one hand, and Mercurial mendacity on the other.

The Meaning of a Balladeer on a London Stage in 1610

Shakespeare builds anticipation around Autolycus's spectacular entrance to the sheepshearing festival by having a servant deliver an enthusiastic introductory description loaded with very specific visual and aural detail, a method of characterization that offers some perspective on the character's expected theatrical effect. The passage is worth quoting in full:

> SERVANT. O, master, if you did but hear the pedlar at the door you would never dance again after a tabor and pipe; no, the bagpipe could not move you. He sings several tunes faster than you'll tell money; he utters them as he had eaten ballads, and all men's ears grew to his tunes.
>
> CLOWN. He could never come better; he shall come in. I love a ballad but even too well, if it be doleful matter merrily set down, or a very pleasant thing indeed, and sung lamentably.
>
> SERVANT. He hath songs for man or woman of all sizes—no milliner can so fit his customers with gloves. He has the prettiest love songs for maids, so without bawdry, which is strange, with such delicate burdens of dildos and fadings, "jump her and thump her"; and where some stretch-mouthed rascal would, as it were, mean mischief and break a foul gap into the matter, he makes the maid to answer, "Whoop, do me no harm, good man"—puts him off, slights him, with "Whoop, do me no harm, good man."
>
> POLIXENES. This is a brave fellow.
>
> CLOWN. Believe me, thou talkest of an admirable conceited fellow. Has he any unbraided wares?
>
> SERVANT. He hath ribbons of all the colours i'th' rainbow; points, more than all the lawyers in Bohemia can learnedly handle, though they come to him by th' gross; inkles, caddises, cambrics, lawns—why, he sings 'em over as they were gods or goddesses. You

> would think a smock were a she-angel, he so chants to the sleeve-hand and the work about the square on't.
>
> (4.4.183–213)

The merchandise made available by the "pedlar" at the door falls into two basic categories: broadside ballads, which he also performs, and a selection of decorative trinkets, including ribbon ("inkles," "caddises") and fine linen ("cambrics," "lawns"). Würzbach notes that combination peddler-balladeers on this model was a familiar fixture at rural gatherings such as the Shepherd's sheepshearing festival, events that offered them an opportunity to hawk their wares to an isolated, relatively undiscerning pool of consumers.[21] In contrast, the balladeers in the city had to compete with a far greater array of amusements, and therefore tended to focus on ballads exclusively rather than offering a diverse range of items for sale. In a thoughtful essay that considers *The Winter's Tale* in relation to news from the Low Countries, Andrew Fleck argues that the association between ballads and ephemeral merchandise connects to a thematic emphasis on the frivolous, material dimension of commercial news: "Owning a piece of printed news lines up with other luxurious commodities—laces, points, gloves—against which moralists had often inveighed in complaining that a decadent English populace lusted after ephemera. Shakespeare associates the news with other meaningless trinkets in Autolycus's efforts to make a profit through a 'silly cheat[ing]' of the gullible masses."[22] This pattern of association is evident in the servant's marked use of language deriving from tradespeople and everyday economic exchange. For example, he tells his master that the peddler "sings several tunes faster than you'll tell money" (performs ballads faster than you can count money), and that "He hath songs for man or woman of all sizes—no milliner can so fit his customers with gloves." As Fleck suggests, there is an element of satiric reduction in these claims, an evocation of popular scorn for the perceived vacuity of news culture: like a pair of fancy gloves or a lacy garter, ballads are nothing more than a fashionable waste of money, a silly thing appealing to the silly tastes of silly people.

But in order to fully grasp how a connection between balladry and frivolous merchandise could function as a comment on news, it is necessary to consider the content and material condition of ballads in much closer detail. As noted above, the documents were printed on single folio sheets, a form of publication typically reserved for texts aimed at a mass market. Dimensions could vary, but most sheets measured somewhere close to 290 mm by 340 mm, or roughly the same dimensions as a standard sheet of A3 paper (portable, but also suitable for pinning up on a tavern wall). A typical ballad would feature a title that stretches across the top of the page, a woodcut illustration, and approximately one hundred lines of rhymed verse in bold, easy-to-read, blackletter type. For an early modern, this style of presentation was the quintessence of popular print. As Würzbach notes, the typeface functioned as a clear indication of the balladeer's designated market: blackletter went out of fashion in the mid-sixteenth century, and, by the seventeenth century, remained in use strictly for texts of a popular or "lowbrow" nature.[23] The price, one halfpenny, was similarly humble—seventeenth-century Londoners could purchase a half loaf of bread, a candle, or a pot of ale for the same amount. In a significant number of cases, the content of ballads connected, in one way or another, to events of a topical nature. Shaaber notes that the character and quality of news content in such ballads was consistent with the character and quality of the documents' material properties:

> Normally a news-ballad is not so much a record of events as a commentary upon them; it is not a harbinger of news but a follower in its wake, expressing the opinion of the mass of the people about it. That it served to some extent, nevertheless, to give currency to the news is not to be doubted, but its own substance is chiefly emotional rather than literal. A ballad on the queen's opening of Parliament is likely to be not so much a description of what took place as an enthusiastic huzza for the most famous, gracious, wise, and splendid of sovereigns and a sincere testimonial of loyalty; a ballad on the French king's defeat of the league will probably have little to say about military operations, but it will be sure to emit a crow of triumph over the discomfiture of the pope and to warn England against Catholic machinations; a ballad on a flood in the north may very well omit all but the meagrest particulars, but it will not fail to expatiate plentifully on this evidence of God's mercy in chastening the sinful or to exhort his people to repentance.[24]

In short, ballads presented information on topical themes in a bold, emotionally charged style calculated to appeal to as wide an audience as possible. With this point in mind, it is important to remember that the form had a built-in performative dimension that set it apart from most other ways of accessing and thinking about the news. For the most part, a ballad was not the sort of thing one read to oneself in private for the sole purpose of acquiring new knowledge. People *sang* ballads out loud and in groups, collectively imagining the grand events described and laughing together over the frequently bawdy humor. A printed ballad, in other words, was much more than a vehicle for information: it was the script for an affective experience, a highly accessible means by which ordinary people at large could tap into the excitement and fashionableness of news culture. As Shaaber suggests, this fundamental purpose meant that balladry as a genre tended to emphasize feelings and popular appeal over factual detail. The point of purchasing a ballad was to get a sense, however vague or distorted, of what people were talking about, to participate in an ongoing public conversation.[25] Factuality mattered to a limited extent, but it was definitely subordinate to fashion. This hierarchy of values represented a stark inversion of what news is putatively all about. As I argued in the previous chapter, one of the chief defining properties of any news item is that, at the very least, it pretends to be true, and the claim of truthfulness is its ostensible source of value. In the case of ballads, however, fashion, not substance, was quite obviously the dominant source of appeal—an aspect the form shared with other mass-market goods, such as fancy gloves and lacy garters. By emphasizing the connection between ballads and ephemeral merchandise, Shakespeare puts his finger on a central tension underlying the production of commercial news: truth only really matters insofar as it relates to salability, which, when one looks beneath the surface, is the ultimate reason for news products to exist in the first place.

As noted, the peddler-balladeer described by the servant has a merchandising style deriving from rural, rather than urban, areas. On the other hand, however, the description also features significant markers connecting the figure to the city—especially London. For example, it is entirely possible that some spectators at the original performances of *The Winter's Tale* had watched a balladeer singing a version of "Whoop, do me no harm!" while they waited to get inside the Globe.[26] As Rollins notes, balladeers were a ubiquitous feature of the urban landscape, particularly common in places such as "the doors of theatres, . . . markets, fairs, bear baitings, taverns, ale-houses, wakes or any other places where a crowd could gather."[27] Indeed, as early as 1579, Stephen Gosson, a former actor turned antitheatrical crusader, complained that London "is so full of vnprofitable Pipers and Fidlers, that a man can no soner enter a tauerne, but two or three caste of them hang at his heeles, to giue him a daunce before he departe."[28] I want to put special emphasis on the pervasive presence of balladeers in London in order to recapture a sense of how sharply Autolycus stands out from among the other characters in the play. Shakespeare uses the servant's introductory description to very purposefully cue recognition of a salient anachronism: the "pedlar" who arrives at the sheepshearing festival on the pastoral Bohemian seacoast is in fact an everyday figure lifted from the streets of London, a figure prominently connected to the economic and discursive situation of the theater itself rather than the romanticized, fictional spaces where the action purportedly plays out. Like the news he trades on, the balladeer is fundamentally a product of a common present.

Now, referring to ballads as "news," as I have been doing, implies a very particular point of view that I want to articulate as clearly as possible before moving on to the mock ballads (or news parodies) at the center of my analysis. An instructive point of reference in this regard is a recent article in which Angela McShane-Jones argues that the term "news-ballad" is historically inaccurate:

> There was no such thing as a "news-ballad." Contemporaries did not use this term. "Ballad" was one of the few stable generic terms appearing in the Stationers registers and content, format or style made no distinction. "News-ballad" was a term constructed by commentators so that they could impose their aesthetic and anachronistic judgments on the broadside ballad. The political ballad was not a failed newspaper, it was poetry, if often only failed poetry, and song. . . . Political ballads were not the "mass journalism" of the people—they were the street and alehouse theatre, the poetry and the counselors of the people—and not just those without the discretion to know any better. . . . The ballad functioned primarily as entertainment, instruction, comment, explanation and complaint, not as a vehicle for information. Ballads depended upon and participated in an already informed and widespread debate about state affairs.[29]

I have no disagreement whatsoever with McShane-Jones's argument, as far as it goes, but I want to point out a few key differences between her approach and my own that will help to bring my notion of ballads and news culture into sharper relief. First, McShane-Jones is writing about a period from around 1550 (when broadside ballads began to appear) up until the end of the seventeenth century. My own focus, on the other hand, centers specifically on 1610–11, the period when *The Winter's Tale* premiered at the Globe. At this time, familiar modern aspects of news culture such as "newspapers," "journalism," and a "press" did not exist in any recognizable form. Indeed, as I argued in chapter 1, the very notion of publicity itself was in a state of intense transformation. What did exist, however, is what I have called the "conceptual foundation" of news culture, a fluid set of ideas, values, things, and practices surrounding an incipient idea of news that did not really begin to come into its own until the 1620s. Although ballads may not have been an early manifestation of the modern newspaper, as McShane-Jones correctly points out, they were nevertheless a significant element of a burgeoning discursive cluster, or ecology, that also included forms such as pamphlets, manuscript newsletters, oral transmission, sermons, and theater—the mechanisms that people "thought with" throughout the process of conceptualizing what news would become. In seeking to correct the anachronistic foisting of balladry into the history of the newspaper, McShane-Jones's argument mitigates what the present analysis endeavors to affirm: the very significant role ballads and balladeers played in cultivating the idea of news itself (this, of course, is the same point that my larger argument makes in regard to the theater).

Second, McShane-Jones writes that the ballad "functioned primarily as entertainment, instruction, comment, explanation and complaint, not as a vehicle for information" and that it "depended upon and participated in an already informed and widespread debate about state affairs." Again, I think this point is essentially correct, but I would add that the same could be said, to varying degrees, about all other news forms in the first decade of the seventeenth century. The closest thing to a straightforward "vehicle of information" in the period was probably the manuscript newsletter (and commercial reproductions thereof), but, even in these documents, there was very little formal distance between ostensibly pure information and elements such as "entertainment, instruction, comment, explanation and complaint." The standard, objective-sounding aesthetic that we associate with news today was in its infancy during Shakespeare's time, and existed alongside a number of other nascent conventions for establishing a semblance of authenticity and authority. People in early modernity *expected* news media to entertain, instruct, comment, explain, and complain—such functions were a normative, inseparable aspect of information delivery (and continue to play an important role in how people think about the news today). McShane-Jones's argument implies that there were "pure" news forms, such as modern newspapers, at the foundation of a discursive scene that "secondary" forms, such as ballads and theater, "depended upon and participated in." But in 1610, the situation was in fact far murkier and far less hierarchical. Ballads may have depended, to a certain extent, on a conversation initiated by other forms of news, but, by the same token, that very conversation itself depended on the public discursive spaces opened up by forms such as balladry and theater, spaces where the values, attitudes, and conventions underlying the idea of news could develop and become manifest in a critical perspective. In short, the crux of the difference between McShane-Jones's approach and my own is that, while she views balladry as an essentially secondary, relatively minor form of news dissemination, I view it as an important aspect of the news culture and a significant progenitor of the modern idea of news.

Setting differences of approach aside, I also want to consider some of the interpretive implications for *The Winter's Tale* foregrounded by McShane-Jones's evocative description of ballads as "street and alehouse theatre." As noted above, the printed document that one received upon purchasing a ballad was in fact only the material token of a much larger experience that included the professional performance of the ballad by the balladeer himself as well as the amateur performances that the consumer could conduct among friends in taverns or private homes. This business model hinged on the same basic marketing strategy employed by pitchmen throughout the ages: the vendor provides a demonstrative performance in order to attract consumers' attention, hoping to sell them a product they can use to reproduce the performance on their own. Making a similar comparison, Würzbach notes that "the balladmonger was his own manager and dependent on his performance of the ballad for success. . . . There was a large and diverse selection of ballads on offer, especially in London, and this required of him the high degree of persuasive power and skill of a present-day salesman in order to arouse people's interest and attract their attention."[30] A detailed study of the continuities between balladry and theater falls outside the scope of my focus of study, but it will suffice, for the purposes of the present argument, to simply point out that a significant portion of the value built into both forms rested with what one might call a "theatrical" performance (in the very general sense of the word "theatrical"). Pushing the argument into more speculative territory, I would add that the two forms almost certainly involved overlapping performance styles and skill sets—to say nothing of their shared pool of potential consumers. In short, the balladeers and the players were competitors: they sold the same basic product (theatrical performance) to the same people (Londoners at large) for more or less the same price (ballads cost a halfpenny, entrance to the Globe was twice as much). These similarities help to explain the title of Gosson's famous antitheatrical invective, which lumps players and balladeers together as equally pestiferous "Caterpillars of a Commonwealth."[31] In view of the threat to theatrical value that such rhetoric could pose, I want to suggest that the representation of balladry in *The Winter's Tale* works in opposition to antitheatrical attitudes, and in conjunction with an ongoing effort to raise the artistic and social profile of commercial drama.[32] With the character of Autolycus, Shakespeare posits an implicit assertion of difference that purposefully sets his own art apart from (and above) balladry. Plucked off the street corner and folded into a full-blown theatrical performance, Autolycus becomes manifest from a critical distance, a position that brings his faults into sharp focus, but, on a more subtle level, also deflects accusations of similar faults away from the commercial theater.[33] By inviting the audience at the Globe to think of themselves as separate from and more discerning than the oafish yokels clamoring to purchase ballads, Shakespeare powerfully underlines the qualitative differences between commercial theater and balladry—the very differences that Gosson's antitheatrical rhetoric sought to obscure.

Ballads, Pamphlets, Monstrous Births, and Singing Fish

Shortly after the servant's enthusiastic introduction, Autolycus enters in disguise singing about the wares he has for sale. The exact tune for this song is unknown, but it seems to be an adaptation from the "cries of London" genre associated with contemporary peddlers and balladeers:[34]

Lawn as white as driven snow,
Cypress black as ere was crow,
Gloves as sweet as damask roses,
Masks for faces and for noses,
Bugle-bracelet, necklace amber;
Perfume for a lady's chamber,
Golden coifs and stomachers
For my lads to give their dears;
Pins and poking-sticks of steel,

What maids lack from head to heel.
Come buy of me, come. Come buy, come buy,
Buy, lads, or else your lasses cry. Come buy.

(4.4.220–29)

Picking up on a motif that began with the servant's description, the song runs through a dense list of exotic-sounding, luxury merchandise, including two types of fine linen ("lawn" and "cypress"), gloves, masks, bracelets, necklaces, perfume, "golden coifs" (a gold-colored, tight-fitting cap), "stomachers" (ornamental garments worn around the waist), pins, and "poking-sticks" (long rods used to stiffen ruffs). As is the case with virtually everything else that Autolycus says in the scene, the song is also dense with potential for bawdy double-entendre: "glove" and "a lady's chamber" were both common euphemisms for "vagina," while "pins," "poking sticks," and "what maids lack" were among the myriad substitutions for "penis." On a similar note, "masks for noses" suggests accessories worn to conceal the nasal deformation that resulted from syphilis—a fleeting, but visually evocative reference that connects to an ongoing pattern of association between an inability to smell and an inability to discern the truth.[35] By slyly dropping this very powerful image into the mix, Autolycus simultaneously hints at his audience's credulity as well as their sexual prurience, aspects that become increasingly apparent as the scene develops. On a related note, the explicitly feminine nature of the merchandise connects to a thematic emphasis on the falsity of women and their appetite for anything fanciful and frivolous—such as "tales."[36] The most prominent manifestation of this pattern occurs in the conversation between Mamillius and Hermione that gives the play its name (2.1.1–32), but there are many further examples, including Leontes's reference to the testimony of midwives as "false / As o'erdyed blacks, as wind, as waters" (1.2.131–32) and Paulina's characterization of Leontes's deluded fantasies as "green and idle" to a point where they would not even meet the (maximally low) standards for belief required by "girls of nine" (3.2.178–79). In short, the song projects a thematically resonant scene of transmission notable for its frivolity, gullibility, lechery and—most of all—femininity. These are the qualities that Shakespeare wants to assign to the market for ballads and, on a more general level, to the market for news.

"Lawn as white" sets the table for one of the very earliest instances of parodic news in English literature: Autolycus's description of two mock news-ballads for the Shepherd's son (Clown) and two country maids

(Mopsa and Dorcas). The first, a send-up of the "monstrous birth" story, is about a usurer's wife who gave birth to twenty moneybags. The second, a send-up of the "prodigy" story, is about a singing fish that appeared in the sky some seventy-three kilometers above sea level.[37] The entire exchange is worth quoting in full:

> CLOWN. What hast here? Ballads?
>
> MOPSA. Pray now, buy some. I love a ballad in print, a-life, for then we are sure they are true.
>
> AUTOLYCUS. Here's one to a very doleful tune, how a usurer's wife was brought to bed of twenty money-bags at a burden, and how she longed to eat adders' heads and toads carbonadoed.
>
> MOPSA. Is it true, think you?
>
> AUTOLYCUS. Very true, and but a month old.
>
> DORCAS. Bless me from marrying a usurer!
>
> AUTOLYCUS. Here's the midwife's name to't, one Mistress Tale-Porter, and five or six honest wives that were present. Why should I carry lies abroad?
>
> MOPSA. [*to Clown*] Pray you now, buy it.
>
> CLOWN. Come on, lay it by, and let's first see more ballads. We'll buy the other things anon.
>
> AUTOLYCUS. Here's another ballad of a fish that appeared upon the coast on Wednesday the fourscore of April forty thousand fathom above water, and sung this ballad against the hard hearts of maids. It was thought she was a woman and was turned into a cold fish, for she would not exchange flesh with one that loved her. The ballad is very pitiful and as true.
>
> DORCAS. Is it true too, think you?
>
> AUTOLYCUS. Five justices' hands at it, and witnesses more than my pack will hold.
>
> (4.4.259–84)

This lighthearted but remarkably complex passage touches on a number of key elements in the popular perception of news culture. I want to point out six basic features. First, there is a claim of currency ("but a month-old"). Second, there is the indiscriminate, insatiable hunger of consumers, expressed here by Mopsa, whose very name is redolent of dimwittedness and a lack of sophistication[38] ("Pray now, buy some"; "Pray you now, buy it"). Third, there is the blatant absurdity and falsity of the news stories on offer. For example, the last name of one of the guarantors for the moneybag ballad is "Tale-Porter" ("lie-teller"), and events in the singing fish ballad purportedly took place on "the fourscore of April" ("April eightieth"). Fourth, there is an almost choric emphasis on truth that brings the problems of veracity in news culture into clear alignment with the play's overarching thematic focus on problems of knowledge and belief ("Is it true, think you?" . . . "very true" . . . "The ballad is very pitiful and as true" . . . "Is it true too, think you?"). Of particular note in this regard is Mopsa's overwrought association between print and truth, which ironically reverses the low reputation of printed news in relation to the more trustworthy manuscript newsletters circulated privately among men of the upper classes ("I love a ballad in print, a-life, for then we are sure they are true"). As Cressy notes, ballads and other commercially printed news forms were "notorious for interlacing lies and truth," a problem that producers attempted to compensate for by prominently working the word "true" or "certain" into titles ("*The true form and shape*" . . . "*The true description*" . . . "*A most certain report*" . . . "*A true and certain relation*" etc.).[39] Mopsa's statement suggests that she takes such claims at face value, without any suspicion of guile. Fifth, there is a satiric focus on authentication that foregrounds the impossibility of ever absolutely establishing the veracity of any given report, another very clear example of how the scene dovetails with thematic concerns in the main plot of the play ("Here's the midwife's name to't, one Mistress Tale-Porter, and five or six honest wives" that were present" . . . "Five justices' hands at it, and witnesses more than my pack will hold"). Sixth (and finally) there is also a satiric focus on patterns of interpretation—the lessons putatively suggested in the text, but also inferred by consumers. For example, Dorcas interprets the moneybag ballad as marriage advice ("Bless me from marrying a usurer!"), and Autolycus interprets the fish ballad as a warning against sexual diffidence ("It was thought she was a woman and was turned into a cold fish, for she would not exchange flesh with one that loved her").

With all of these features in view, I want to argue that the focus of Shakespeare's satiric interrogation in the passage is not only on balladry, but also on the fundamental concepts underlying the developing idea of news itself. As noted, the mock ballads are send-ups of the "monstrous birth" story and the "prodigy" story, overlapping genres that featured heavily in ballads, but derived from the inexpensive, blackletter news pamphlets that began to appear around the middle of the sixteenth century. Like the mock ballads sold by Autolycus, these documents were notable for subject matter of a sensational nature, dubious claims of veracity, an emphasis on currency, and an interpretive framework that encouraged addressees to infer an instructive purpose. More importantly, as part of their authentication apparatus, they regularly included the names of corroborating witnesses—a salient aspect of Autolycus's ballads that was *not* a typical feature of actual ballads in the period (it is rather difficult to make a list of witnesses rhyme).[40] This detail is especially important, I suggest, because it shows that the satiric focus of the mock ballads is not on balladry alone. Autolycus's reference to "Mistress Tale-Porter" and the "five or six honest wives," purportedly ensuring the veracity of the moneybag ballad, would have put Shakespeare's audience in mind of commercial news in general, not just balladry, and the same is true for the "five justices" (judges), and numerous other witnesses that he refers to in his description of the fish ballad. As noted above, by suggesting that these figures of authentication are no more real than the phony reports they supposedly guarantee, Shakespeare puts pressure on one of the fundamental conceits in the developing idea of news: the notion that the name of a person in a printed document was a reliable indication of veracity. Ultimately, the most prominent point of the mock ballads is that any given news report could be false, regardless of corroboration, because corroboration itself is as easy to falsify as anything else. Any prospective news consumer had to come to terms with the inescapable impossibility of ever establishing the absolute truth of any given report—the same problem that bedevils Leontes in the main plot of the play.

A brief examination of a contemporary news pamphlet will help to bring the historical context of Shakespeare's critique into clearer focus. For a representative example of a "monstrous birth" story, consider *Strange Nevves out of Kent* (1609), a fourteen-page pamphlet that became available at London bookstalls around the same time that Shakespeare was writing *The Winter's Tale*. Following a standard pattern for the genre, the document begins by establishing an interpretive framework that posits the event as an instance of divine signification: "God we see is highly offended with vs, in that hee thus changeth the secret workings of nature, as he lately shewed, in the strange birth of a monstrous childe brought into the World, at Sandwitch in Kent."[41] This introduction is followed by a detailed list of six witnesses ("1. *M. Bills*, at the signe of the Shippe in Thames streete. 2. *M. Dickson*, a Cooper, in Thames streete, neere to Saint Dunstons church," etc.) and a report about an anonymous pregnant woman who sought shelter at the home of an old widow, went into labor shortly thereafter, and eventually gave birth to a severely deformed, stillborn child.[42] The main part of the story consists of an extensive, two-page description of the disfigured corpse and the horrified reaction of the witnesses present, putting particular emphasis on grim details such as the child's shrunken legs and the "earthly"[43] stench that filled the room. With its fundamental purpose thereby accomplished, the document concludes by reiterating the introductory assertions of divine significance and by making note of some recent phenomena along similar lines. One of these items presents another, unexpected, parallel to *The Winter's Tale:* "London had lately a feareful patterne of the same, by a huge deformed fish, that would groane and roare contrary to his kind, which by many people was seene at the Swanne within Newgate."[44] I have not been able to locate any other contemporary references to this prodigious, roaring, and groaning fish (apparently exhibited at an inn in central London), but the factuality of the marvel is less important to me than the fact of the story itself—or more precisely, the fact that "vocalizing fish" stories were "in the news" at the time.[45] Could this be the inspiration for the singing fish in Shakespeare's second mock ballad? Did the dramatist have *Strange Nevves out of Kent* on his desk as he wrote? Although I find the possibility tantalizing, I am reluctant to presume a direct connection. Nevertheless, as noted, I think it is unquestionably significant that such stories were actually circulating in London at the time, and that people seem to have understood them in more or less the same way that Autolycus and his audience understand the mock ballads.[46] The moneybag ballad and the singing fish ballad are not merely silly, lighthearted absurdities inserted for the sake of levity: they are part of a very specific, critically acute analysis of the assumptions and interpretive practices underlying the developing idea of news.

Shakespeare and the Problem of Belief

The foregoing analysis has shown how a detailed, comprehensive engagement with news-thinking in *The Winter's Tale* 4.4 lines up with news-thinking throughout the Shakespearean corpus and contemporary discourse in general. In addition to restoring the historical significance of allusions to specific elements in news culture—such as the *Mercurius Gallobelgicus*, ballads, balladeers, and news pamphlets—I have presented a picture of how the scene significantly resituates the attitudes, practices, tensions, and assumptions at the center of the new idea of news. If we step back, the element that appears most prominently in this picture is a wide-ranging meditation on news and truth: how news manufactures a semblance of authority and truthfulness, and how the projection of that idealized self-image works in conjunction with the production of a salable commodity. On a similar note, there is also a very severe, unflattering look at the news public, their credulity, their indiscriminate voracity, their lurid tastes, their lack of sophistication, their obsession with fashion, their disregard for substance, and so on, that pushes serious questions about the very notion of publicity itself into the foreground. Less prominently, but of particular importance to the present analysis, the scene also registers an uneasy recognition of the very close relationship between commercial news and the theater. As Rumor points out at the beginning of *2 Henry IV*, the two forms catered to essentially the same public—a new social entity that they also helped to create. Shakespeare wants to put some distance between himself and unsavory, public panderers such as Autolycus, but on the other hand, he also wants to co-opt them by folding the raw appeals of news culture into his own drama. Satiric derision notwithstanding, Autolycus is, at face value, a figure of tremendous appeal—a begrudging testament to the undeniable attraction of news.

With these elements in place, I now want to develop a perspective on how Shakespeare's analysis of news culture fits into his larger philosophical project for *The Winter's Tale*, and, in so doing, provide some perspective on how the problems of knowledge pertaining to the new idea of news fits within a much larger movement in the history of ideas. As noted in the introduction, *The Winter's Tale* is an extended meditation on truth and belief: how to evaluate the truthfulness of any given reality, how to know what to believe, how to accommodate uncertainty. It is by now clear how these questions apply to Autolycus and the mock ballads he purveys. For a general idea of how they apply to the main plot of the play, consider the following thoughts on 4.4 from Stephen Orgel:

> Autolycus' ability to produce documentary confirmations of the most fantastic of [the mock ballads'] claims provides a wry commentary on the questions of evidence that fill the play. The ballads serve, indeed, as indices to the nature of and capacity for belief, rustic models for all those events that are said to be like incredible old tales—Antigonus' fatal encounter with the bear, Perdita's reappearance, Hermione's restoration, *The Winter's Tale* itself—but must nevertheless be believed. They are also prototypes of Paulina's equally unlikely but pre-eminently artistic charade at the play's conclusion, for which she requires that "You do awake your faith"—requires what in any

> other context would be called gullibility. Autolycus is as essential a part of that conclusion as Paulina.[47]

Framing Orgel's reading in slightly different terms, one might say that the characters in *The Winter's Tale* repeatedly find themselves confronted with reports that elicit the same basic questions that Autolycus endeavors to answer in the process of selling his ballads: "Is it true?" and "How do you know?"—questions that one can only ever answer indirectly by referring back to the report itself or to another report, questions that one can always ask again and again without ever arriving at an absolutely conclusive answer. The primary example of this pattern is of course King Leontes, whose refusal (or inability) to believe assertions of Hermione's faithfulness and Mamillius's paternity leads to an accelerated narrowing of the grounds for belief in general. Convinced of the certainty of his own delusions, he categorically rejects all forms of contravening evidence—Hermione's oaths, the testimony of midwives, the assurances of his advisors, even physical resemblance—on the basis that it could potentially be a fabrication no more real than the witnesses supposedly guaranteeing the veracity of Autolycus's mock ballads. What the play as a whole presents, as Orgel suggests, is something along the lines of a spectrum of belief, with the solipsistic skepticism of Leontes on one end and the infinite credulity of Mopsa and Dorcas on the other.

The preeminent explication of this dimension of the play is the chapter on *The Winter's Tale* in Stanley Cavell's *Disowning Knowledge*, a study that aligns Shakespearean drama with writers such as Montaigne and Descartes, thereby placing it within the context of the epistemological turn brought about by the Reformation and the revival of classical skepticism during the sixteenth century. Cavell reads Leontes's insane jealousy at the beginning of the play as "a portrait of the skeptic at the moment of the world's withdrawal from his grasp," a dramatic situation that he also finds at the center of plays such as *Lear*, *Othello*, and *Hamlet*:

> Leontes' first question to his son is: "Art thou my boy?" And then he goes on to try to recognize the boy as his by their resemblance in certain marks and features, at first by comparing their noses. That speech, distracted, ends with a repetition of the earlier doubt: "Art thou my calf?" Already here we glimpse Shakespearean pathos, a sense that one may feel mere sadness enough to fill an empty world. Upon the repetition Leontes compares their heads. These efforts are of course to no avail. Then he rules out the value of the testimony of

> anyone else, as if testifying that he must know for himself; and as he proceeds he insists that his doubts are reasonable, and he is led to consider his dreams. It is all virtually an exercise out of Descartes's *Meditations*. But while Descartes suggests that his doubts may class him with madmen, he succeeds (for some of his readers) in neutralizing the accusation, that is, in sufficiently establishing the reasonableness of his doubts, at least provisionally. Whereas Leontes is, while in doubt, certainly a madman.[48]

Like Orgel, Cavell links Leontes's crisis of doubt to a recurring commentary on the believability of reported events. The most prominent of these comments are the three points (four if you count the title) where a direct comparison is made between a "tale" and the events of the play itself: Rogero on Perdita's return ("This news, which is / called true, is so like an old tale that the verity of it is in / strong suspicion," 5.2.27–29), the Steward on Antigonus's death ("Like an old tale still, which will have matter to / rehearse though credit be asleep and not an ear open / —he was torn to pieces with a bear," 5.2.60–62), and Paulina on Hermione's resurrection ("That she is living, / Were it but told you, should be hooted at / Like an old tale," 5.3.115–17). As Cavell points out, in all three cases, the underlying purpose of the comparison is to draw attention to the difficulty of believing without seeing, or in other words, the difficulty of ever knowing with absolute certainty whether any given narrated event is true.[49] The same pattern also applies to the wide variety of narrated events that exhibit problems of provenance in one way or another—a long series of potential "tales" that repeatedly leave the door open for the same sort of skeptical vertigo that troubles Leontes. Autolycus's ballads fit this pattern perfectly, as I have shown. Other key examples include the story of Hermione's return, which comes together as a group of excited gossipers swap secondhand scraps of information (5.2.1–110) and the very complicated backstory for the oracular proclamation, which purportedly travels from Apollo, to a priestess, to a scribe, to a scroll, to Cleomenes and Dion, to the officer who reads it aloud at Hermione's trial, increasing the potential for corruption at every turn (3.1.1–22; 3.2.10–30).[50] Perhaps most importantly, there is also Paulina's story surrounding the statue that supposedly comes to life, a fabrication that Leontes must nevertheless accept in order to end his own story on a note of happiness and redemption—a suggestion, perhaps, that belief does not always have to be entirely rational in order to be meaningful and valuable.[51] By bringing news culture into connection with all of these other ways of thinking about truth and belief, Shakespeare puts the questions presented by the new idea of news into a broad, intellectually and emotionally robust perspective that the theater, above all other forms of publicity at the time, was uniquely able to provide.

"Times News" and New Forms of Knowledge

Cavell's alignment of Shakespearean drama with Cartesian skepticism brings me to some final observations about the innovative contribution of news and theater to seventeenth-century thought. By way of conclusion, I want to suggest that both forms inherently endorsed a new way of knowing that was only beginning to count as knowledge, a new sort of truth that was only beginning to count as true. Cavell's analysis is instructive in this regard because, although his argument for Shakespeare's general affinity to Descartes is easy to agree with, he misses a key point of departure between the two thinkers: unlike Descartes, Shakespeare was not a foundationalist—that is to say, he did not subscribe to a theory of knowledge positing a core foundation of absolutely certain, immutable beliefs as the basis for discerning truth. On the contrary, the epistemological framework for Shakespeare's poetry and plays in fact has much more in common with the reinvented idea of truth cultivated by news culture (see chapter 1), an idea of truth that was not atemporal or absolute, but mutable and subject to the ongoing brokering of interpretive communities. As I argued in regard to news, this way of thinking about truth was not simply a matter of abstract philosophical argumentation on Shakespeare's part, but more like a conceptual accommodation that evolved naturally out of the material conditions and value-making practices of the early modern theater.[52]

My understanding of antifoundationalism in Shakespeare owes a significant debt to Lars Engle's *Shakespearean Pragmatism: Market of His Time*, a study that aligns the dramatist with post-Cartesian, pragmatic thinkers such as John Dewey and, more recently, Richard Rorty, attributing to Shakespeare "both a view of social interaction as an economy, a diffuse network of discursive transactions which hang together according to humanly established (and thus mutable) patterns of exchange, and a tendency to treat truth, knowledge, and certainty as relatively stable goods in such an economy rather than gateways out of it."[53] This argument functions as a corrective to Cavell, whose analysis, in Engle's view, goes too far in its identification of Shakespeare with Descartes: "In arguing that

Shakespeare's texts tend to pose problems in collective economic terms, I move them out of the arena of radical skepticism (the solitary knower's difficulties with certainty) and into that of pragmatism (the involved participant's struggle to maintain a satisfactory position in an ongoing pattern of exchanges)."[54] Beginning with the *Sonnets*, Engle's interpretation of Shakespeare brings into focus "a peculiarly de-idealized or anti-Platonic notion of how things hang together: a world-view in which truth and lasting value are simply that which a mutable community, for a variety of discussable reasons, chooses to regard as good for a long time." In Sonnet 108, for example, there is a notion of poetry triumphing over time (but not transcending it) by "offering a repeatable gesture that will serve recurrent human needs," and in Sonnet 123 "a claim not to independence [from time] but, rather, to continually recovered contingent success."[55] For another fairly straightforward example that applies the same interpretive methodology to drama, consider Engle's reading of Ulysses's speech from *Troilus and Cressida* 3.3., wherein the wily commander warns Achilles that he must constantly renew proof of his greatness if he does not want his public reputation to diminish: "Let not virtue seek / Remuneration for the thing it was; / For beauty, wit, / High birth, vigour of bone, desert in service, / Love, friendship, charity, are subjects all / To envious and calumniating Time" (3.3.170–75). As in his analysis of the *Sonnets*, Engle finds in these lines an expression of a "market ethic," a pragmatic attitude toward value characterized by a "general redescription of fixed systems as dynamic economies"—a manner of looking at the world that regards truth, not as an irreducible absolute, but as a mutable (but relatively stable) property entirely contingent on human consensus (not unlike Achilles' reputation).[56]

The contingent, time-bound notion of truth attributed by Engle to Shakespeare brings me back around to *The Winter's Tale*, a play about truth and belief that features the traditional figure Father Time, serving as Chorus, at the beginning of the fourth act. Turning an hourglass over to show that the performance has reached the halfway point, Time asks the audience to excuse the sixteen-year gap between the first part of the story and the second—a break in the narrative that blatantly disregards the neoclassical standard (derived from Aristotle) stipulating that the fictional time-frame of a dramatic production should not exceed twenty-four hours:

Impute it not a crime
To me or my swift passage that I slide

O'er sixteen years, and leave the growth untried
Of that wide gap, since it is in my power
To o'erthrow law, and in one self-born hour
To plant and o'erwhelm custom. Let me pass
The same I am ere ancient'st order was,
Or what is now received. I witness to
The times that brought them in; so shall I do
To th' freshest things now reigning, and make stale
The glistering of this present as my tale
Now seems to it. Your patience this allowing,
I turn my glass, and give my scene such growing
As you had slept between. (4.1.3–17)

With Engle's analysis in view, it is easy to identify a basic congruity between the concept of time developed in this passage and time as it appears throughout the corpus of Shakespeare's works: like the "ancient'st order" and the "freshest things now reigning," the validity and importance of the Aristotelian standards are subject to human constituency and therefore also subject to a temporal force that can "plant and o'erwhelm" any custom within the space of an hour. All that the Chorus requires, therefore, is the allowance and cooperation of the audience itself—what counts as "good" in drama depends, not on everlasting classical standards, but on mutable standards sustained by ongoing consensus among human beings.[57] It is important to note, however, that in contrast to the "envious and calumniating Time" described by Ulysses in *Troilus and Cressida*, the Chorus's description of temporal force has a patently positive character: Shakespeare straightforwardly celebrates the mutable, publicly developed style of knowing and conferring judgment that enabled cultural producers like himself and his colleagues to carve out a place for themselves in the marketplace.[58] As I have argued, the implicit promotion of this new style of knowing (or form of knowledge) was a key point of confluence between the news trade and the commercial theater.

The Chorus comes close to making this exact point a few lines later. Giving the audience a preview of what they can expect to see in the second half of the play, he hints that Perdita is "now grown in grace / Equal with wondering" (24–25), but stops short of providing any further information in order to "let Time's news / Be known when 'tis brought forth" (26–27). The phrase "Time's news" is significant to the present argument in two respects. First, it presents an idea of news as bound by, and developing in, a temporal context—an idea of news, in other words, as a form of knowledge that requires sustained attention to an ongoing public conversation that changes with the passage of time. Moreover, although the Chorus stands outside the fiction, and although he directs his address to a theatrical audience also outside the fiction, the "news" he hints at (the return of Perdita to Sicilia) is not news in the ordinary sense of the word, but news of a fictional event (the same event, by the way, that Rogero refers to when he says, "This news, which is / called true, is so like an old tale that the verity of it is in / strong suspicion" (5.2.27–29). In effect then, the Chorus is inviting the audience to think about theatrical experience in the same way they think about news, thereby blurring the distinction between the two forms of knowledge and drawing attention to their shared investment in an inherently processual, publicly oriented manner of knowing and thinking about the world.

CHAPTER 3

A Game at Chess and the Making of a Theatrical Public

During the course of a nine-day run in August 1624, Thomas Middleton's *A Game at Chess* attracted thirty thousand spectators, or a seventh of London's adult population, approximately twelve times the regular attendance rate for all of the city's theaters combined.[1] This unprecedented popularity derived from the players' impersonation of contemporary public figures and enactment of political events, a daring innovation that made the convergence of theater and news culture a patent point of attraction. Presented as a conflict between warring black and white pieces on a chessboard, the play dramatizes issues surrounding James I's Spanish policy—particularly Prince Charles's disastrous trip to Spain, the most important news story of the day. The following chapter argues that Middleton's remarkable appropriation and re-mediation of news discourse presents a uniquely detailed example of how drama participated in news culture and helped to develop the idea of news itself. This uniqueness pertains to the remarkable history and news-centeredness of the performance, but also to the uncommonly rich archive of contemporary comment, a record that offers a perspective on the discourse surrounding *Game* as it made, and became, the news.

In addition to developing an important example of theater's contribution to news history, I also hope to offer a sharp argument against the dominant view of *Game* as a jingoistic expression of anti-Catholicism, Hispanophobia, and national pride. As the foregoing chapters have repeatedly pointed out, commercial theater in early modern London created a new sort of discursive space where people could think and feel about matters of mutual concern on a communal, voluntary basis, a space that Lake and Questier describe as "a sort of playpen in which participants could adopt and lay aside, ventriloquise and caricature, try on for size, test and discard a whole variety of subject positions, claims to cultural authority, arguments and counter-arguments about legitimacy and power."[2] Unlike other contemporary forms of mass assembly (sermons, civic pageantry, executions, etc.), theater leaned toward intellectual flexibility and away from dogmatism—it invited people to think together about new things and in new ways, rather than endeavoring to inculcate a specific idea or point of view. This point is particularly important to keep in mind when working through the critical bibliography that has built up around *Game* over the past thirty or so years. Beginning with Margot Heinemann's groundbreaking analysis in the 1980s, interpretations have tended to frame the play in terms of an attempt by individuals within the aristocracy to address a tacitly assumed public sphere. Most notably, Jerzy Limon and Thomas Cogswell have both argued that *Game* disseminated anti-Spanish propaganda under the auspices of a pro-war initiative headed by Prince Charles and the Duke of Buckingham, while in Heinemann's own argument it transmitted propaganda on behalf of a "Puritan Opposition." Arguing against these readings, but making similar assumptions, Trevor Howard-Hill interprets the play as a reflection of nationalistic fervor, an attempt by the author himself to project a monological meaning.[3] In contrast, I develop an analysis that proceeds from a markedly different view of the discursive situation of the early modern theater. Building on the theory of early modern publicity laid out in chapter 1, I begin by recognizing that, while a fully developed public sphere did not exist in early modernity, the period nevertheless involved a significant proliferation of incipient publics and public-making activity. My reading therefore approaches *Game*, not as a vehicle for broadcasting a particular message to an already-constituted public sphere, but as part of a process of *making a public*—a process that becomes apparent, I argue, by attending to how the play connects to other sorts of news-related discursive activity, or in other words, how it brought various people and things into new dialogical relationships. At first glance, this methodology may not seem particularly new: a number of New Historicist (and post–New Historicist) approaches to theater history have arisen out of the basic idea that to study literature or theater in early modern England is to apprehend multiple intersecting discourses. The key distinction here, however, is the focus, not simply on intersection or circulation, but on a process of transposition and concatenation that contributes to the evolution of a public by making discourse available in new ways to new adherents, thereby enabling people to think, interact, and feel together in new ways.[4] This approach allows for analysis better equipped to account for the complexity and interpretive openness of Middleton's social commentary. Rather than making *Game* representative of any single interest or mood, it shows how Hispanophobic, anti-Catholic, or nationalistic elements can meaningfully coexist with elements such as suspicion of the English court and fascination with Catholicism and Spain.[5]

An understanding of the relationship between *Game* and theatrical public making requires attention to the public-making function of transposition. As noted in chapter 1, the connective tissue, or through-line, that enables the grouping of people is a conditioned mode of attention, an understanding among constituents that they are part of the "anyone and everyone" implicitly postulated by nonexclusive, open-ended discourse. One way of thinking about public making, therefore, is as a process of transposition and reorientation: making discourse available in new ways to new adherents in new spaces. In some cases the medium of transposition might be oral, as is the case with a debate or a conversation, while in other cases it can be a made thing, such as a newspaper. The public-making function of made things is particularly important from a historiographical point of view because, unlike straightforward exchange between people, which is ephemeral, exchange orchestrated by a made thing persists, thereby providing a fixed record. In order to study the public created by the early modern theater, therefore, one must look for evidence of transposition—public making—in the made things that facilitate the availability of discourse. As noted above, *Game* is an ideal object of study in this regard because it has left a number of surviving documents that show it generating discourse that moved out of the theater and into a wide variety of spaces, thereby extending the limits of the theatrical public. This collection of documents includes six manuscripts, three quartos, fifteen reports of performances, ten official letters, and Jonson's *The Staple of News*. Conversely, the play also offers a number of examples of movement *into* the theater. Rather than classical literature or history texts, Middleton mined material from inexpensive newssheets, polemical pamphlets, and other media deriving from the public centered on contemporary news. These connections to news culture are particularly significant because they document an evolution in meaning concomitant to publication. As Michael Warner very helpfully makes clear, all public discourse not only postulates, but also characterizes a space of conversation.[6] Attention to the ways that the meaning of discourse evolves as it moves from one space to another enables a specification of this process of characterization, thereby making it possible to construct a profile of a public-making practice in distinctive detail. With this goal in mind, my methodology therefore regards the set of contemporary texts related to *Game* as the vestiges of publication, a fragmented but nevertheless legible record of a public-making process in action. In what follows, I will draw on this record in an analysis of three salient transpositions, two that involve movement into the theater, and a third that involves movement from the theater to the variety of discursive spaces that made up the theatrical public.

Middleton and News

Before getting to the play itself, however, it is necessary to situate Middleton within the very significant evolution of news culture that occurred in the years between the initial performances of *The Winter's Tale* (1610–11) and *A Game at Chess* (1624). By the mid-1620s, the idea of news had gained something like a critical mass—a rapidly increasing volume of news products, news producers, news consumers, and news discourse had irreversibly transformed the older, more limited conception of news as a discrete, intermittent report, and made way for the broader notion of an ongoing, permanent, publicly accessible conversation among an unknown group of strangers. One of the most prominent factors compelling this new way of thinking about the news was the publishing syndicate set up in the early 1620s by Nathaniel Butter, Nicholas Bourne, and others, an enterprise that made serialized news a regular, easily accessible commodity for the very first time (see chapter 1). As the news public became bigger and more established, it also became more sophisticated (if not wiser), more demanding of elaborate authentication structures, more alert to subtle distinctions of decorum, and even more voracious—a shift that derived force and direction from intense general interest in a few key subjects at the center of popular discourse in the second decade of the seventeenth century. On an international front, the overwhelmingly dominant focus of reports was the long series of battles, intrigues, and diplomatic maneuvers pertaining to the Thirty Years' War (1618–48), a concern that many people in England viewed as a battle between true religion (Protestantism) and the Antichrist

(Catholicism, Rome, and Spain). As far as I can tell, almost every single news story reported in surviving English corantos and periodical newsbooks from 1620 to 1640 connects back to the Thirty Years' War in one way or another.[7] Domestic news, on the other hand, focused extensively (though not entirely) on the increasingly beleaguered court of James I, which became the subject of significant disapproval in connection to the Thomas Overbury affair (a key referent for *The Witch*) and the king's intimate, and very high-profile, relationships with a series of younger men, particularly the Duke of Buckingham. Because of its politically sensitive nature, news of court scandal tended to rely especially heavily on noncommercial, surreptitious mechanisms of transmission such as private newsletters, anonymous verse libels, satirical ballads, gossip, etc.[8] Of course, more oblique mechanisms for representing and thinking about court news played a key role as well, and theater was very important in this regard. By transferring issues to a foreign locale, dramatists created a space where a very sophisticated meditation on courtly corruption could occur. Notable examples include Webster's *The Duchess of Malfi* (originally performed at the Blackfriars in 1612, reprised at the Globe in 1614, and published in 1623), Middleton's *The Witch* (1616), Shakespeare's *Measure for Measure* (originally written in 1603–4, but possibly revised by Middleton in 1621),[9] Middleton's *Women Beware Women* (1621), and Middleton and Rowley's *The Changeling* (1622).

A brief look at *The Witch* will help to introduce the variety of subtle techniques that Middleton used to transpose news discourse to a theatrical context. As noted above, the play bears a significant connection to the Thomas Overbury affair, a scandal that began to unfold in 1613 when James I approved the annulment of Frances Howard's marriage to Robert Devereux so she could marry Robert Carr, the king's favorite—thereby making Howard one of the most notorious women in all of England. As grounds for the annulment, Frances cited her husband's failure to consummate the marriage, a claim she substantiated by submitting to a widely ridiculed examination by ten matrons who found her hymen intact. Devereux admitted his inability to have sex with his wife, but denied charges of impotence, leaving the door open for rumors that Frances had used witchcraft to magically debilitate him in order to get out of the marriage. In 1616, the story grew into an even greater scandal when the court found Frances and her new husband guilty of poisoning Thomas Overbury, a close advisor to Robert Carr and a political enemy of the Howard family. Because of the light it cast on questionable practices in James's inner circle, the trial tarnished his court with the ultimately irreparable stigma of corruption. Twenty years earlier, officials could have exercised greater control over the spread of harmful information, but by 1616, news was much more difficult to curtail. Numerous pamphlets, trial reports, and broadside ballads, as well as noncommercial texts such as private letters and anonymous verse libels appeared in the wake of the trial.[10] This outpouring of responses also included *The Witch*, a supernatural comedy that distributes salient aspects of Frances Carr's story throughout three interrelated plot strands. As Marion O'Connor notes in her edition of the play for *The Oxford Middleton*, the references in *The Witch* to Frances Carr's story "are altogether too insistent and too elaborate to be either accidental or incidental" (1125).[11] They include an unconsummated marriage, a selectively impotent husband, the intervention of a powerful uncle (an analogue for James I), a poisoning, and, as the title suggests, connections to witchcraft.[12] In addition to these references, a prominent visual link to news sources occurs at 2.2.31–37, when the character Francisca (a name suggestively close to "Frances") gratuitously contemplates her reflection in a mirror, thereby evoking a strong visual parallel with an iconic portrait of Carr from the 1615 broadsheet ballad, *Mistress Turner's Farewell to All Women* (O'Connor 1125).[13] The subtlety and variety of these connections to the dominant domestic news story of the day provides a revealing early example of the techniques Middleton would apply again in the transpositions from news culture that he brought together in *Game*—transpositions that are at the center of the following analysis.

News from Spain, to Court, to Print, to Stage

The first transposition I want to discuss concerns a popular narrative that framed Charles I's trip to Spain as a heroic voyage of discovery on behalf of European Protestantism. This incredible fabrication grew out of the unique political climate of 1624, a year notable for dramatic reversals in James I's Spanish policy. In order to appreciate the significance attached to these developments, one must keep in mind the larger context of religious trauma stretching back to the previous generation. In the short time between 1530 and 1560, England swung from Catholicism to Protestantism, back to Catholicism, and then back to Protestantism again, leaving the country in a state of spiritual disorientation by the end of the sixteenth century. The Protestant majority feared yet another reversion to Catholicism in 1603 when James assumed the throne—a fear compounded by the lingering threat of assimilation into the Spanish Empire. Although the king remained a Protestant, his toleration of Catholic practices and his close relationship with Catholic foreigners (most notably his own wife) fostered an acute religious paranoia throughout the first few decades of the 1600s. Tensions became particularly sharp in 1617 when he entered into negotiations with Spain to marry his son, Prince Charles, to the Infanta Maria, sister of Felipe IV. This "Spanish Match," as contemporaries knew it, promised to forge a lasting alliance between Protestant England and Catholic Spain, a prospect that appealed to James's diplomatic ambitions, but seemed dangerously naive to a domestic population that proudly remembered the defeat of the Spanish Armada (1588) and the discovery of the Gunpowder Plot (1605) as moments of national triumph over the ever-present threat of Spanish subjugation. James continued to pursue the match for seven years, hoping against odds that Spain might intervene on behalf of his son-in-law, Frederick V (elector of the Palatinate of the Rhine), who lost his hereditary domain to the besieging Holy Roman Empire in 1620 and desperately awaited English military assistance to get it back. Rather than pursuing a religious war on the continent, James continued to do what he could to push the faltering marriage negotiations forward by introducing restraints on anti-Spanish speech and curbing restrictions on the bitterly hated community of Jesuits operating in England at the time. These measures accomplished very little besides adding further tension to the already strained relationship between English Protestants and the throne.

Frustrated by the continued lack of progress in 1623, Prince Charles made a rash bid to expedite negotiations and secure the match once and for all. Accompanied by the Duke of Buckingham (George Villiers), he donned a false beard and traveled on horseback through France in the dead of winter to Madrid to present himself at the Spanish court and claim the Infanta as his bride. Things did not go as planned. Negotiations continued to falter, and Charles remained abroad for almost eight months while England waited anxiously for assurances of his safety. Finally, on 15 October 1623, he returned home—without the Infanta—to the great relief of Protestants across the nation. His homecoming elicited widespread jubilation across England. The bells at Cambridge rang for three days straight, and hundreds of celebratory bonfires burned throughout London. This surge of goodwill set the stage for the series of political reversals and nationalist fervor that distinguishes 1624 from preceding years. In a move calculated to capitalize on public sentiment and cover up the failure and naïveté of the trip to Spain, Buckingham concocted a version of events that cast himself and Charles as religious heroes, crusaders on a mission to oblige the king of Spain to declare his true intentions so that James would give up his hopes for a Spanish match and send forces to rescue the Palatinate from the clutches of Catholicism. He related this "discovery narrative," as I have termed it, in a speech to Parliament on 24 February 1624, and, with Charles's help, proceeded to push James toward a much more aggressive Spanish policy that included the expulsion of the Jesuits, the relaxation of restrictions on anti-Spanish speech, and preparations for war in Germany. The new policy provided tremendous relief to the Protestant majority, which celebrated Charles and Buckingham as the founders of a "blessed revolution," a longed-for end to the religious ambivalence that had characterized the king's reign. These events, and the network of meanings attached to them, comprise the historical context and major plot elements for the discovery narrative that Middleton imported into *Game*.[14]

In a landmark study, Thomas Cogswell tracks the circulation of the discovery narrative from Parliament to commonplace books, to newsletters, to polemical pamphlets, and eventually to the theater, arguing that by transmitting the story, *Game* functioned as a vehicle for propaganda:

> The King's Men acted out the broader strokes of Buckingham's romantic account to a daily audience of three thousand. Middleton's play therefore served a critical propaganda function for Charles and Buckingham. *A Game at Chess* offered a plausible justification for the trip as much as it stirred up popular jingoism.[15]

Cogswell's analysis makes a valuable contribution to scholarship on Middleton's sources, but his propaganda argument mistakenly assumes that the transmission of the discovery narrative necessarily involved a wholesale transfer of Buckingham's ideology and purpose. In fact, the exact opposite was the case: when the discovery narrative moved into *Game*, it became part of a multivocal conversation and therefore took on a richer diversity of potential meanings—*Game* reoriented the meaning of the discovery narrative, and not vice versa. As I have argued, the act of public making—making things visible in new ways and from new perspectives to new people in new spaces—has an influence on how and what things mean, and this tendency to complicate meaning, to play meanings off each other, was a particularly prominent aspect of public-making practices in the early modern theater. Middleton effectively depropagandized the discovery narrative by bringing it into conversation with competing viewpoints.

Such viewpoints are not hard to find. As a fundamental feature of design, Middleton uses robust criticism of Catholicism and Spain to telegraph a more subtle critique of the English court, implicitly evoking "common anti-courtier and anti-court stereotypes" that portrayed James's administration as a hotbed of "ambition, flattery, slander, and deceit."[16] Thus, many of the negative qualities exhibited by Black characters appear in White characters as well, but to a lesser degree: the White King is credulous, the White Duke is vain, and the White King's Pawn is a dissembler. These flaws reflect real or perceived faults of actual public figures and invite comparison with the more advanced corruption attributed to Spain. In keeping with theatrical protocol, however, Middleton always makes such connections suggestively, not directly. Although *Game* went further than most drama by actually impersonating public men in performance, it was otherwise entirely typical in terms of the distance posited between playwright and satirical implication. As Bellany notes, calculated detachment enabled dramatists to "represent political issues and yet refrain from seeming to express positive opinions," a technique that turned the conventional view of poetry as "fantastical" discourse to advantage.[17] In a brilliant iteration of this strategy, Middleton shrouds all potentially political significations within a game (the chess allegory), within a dream (Error's dream of the game), within a play (a mode of discourse associated with leisure and fancy), thereby installing a triple buffer against any accusation of satirical intent.

Despite all of this buffering, however, the record of contemporary reception shows that audiences at the Globe were, at the very least, open to the possibility that *Game* might not present an entirely flattering representation of the English court. Eyewitness John Holles called the play "a foule iniury to Spayn [and] no great honor to England,"[18] Amerigo Salvetti noted that it reflected poorly "on those that gave [Gondomar] credence,"[19] and Alvise Valaresso commented on the harm done to the king's reputation "by representing the ease with which he was deceived."[20] These comments attest to the availability (or presumed availability) of irony in Middleton's application of the chess allegory, an aspect of the play explicated in an essay by Richard A. Davies and Alan R. Young from 1976:

> Middleton deliberately departs from the tradition of chess metaphor by fusing the contrasting connotations of the metaphor in such a way as to create moral ambiguity and satiric irony. Superficially, his chosen metaphor posits a well-ordered universe, but a close look at the

> world of the play reveals a lack of moral clarity. The chief characteristic of life as it is lived by the Black and White Houses is dissimulation. If we accept that White is good and Black is evil we fail to perceive the degree of "strange cunning" that constitutes Middleton's typically complex irony.[21]

A strong example of the ambiguity that Davies and Young describe occurs at the end of 5.3, when the White King refers to the White Knight as "Truths glorious masterpiece" (5.3.2190)[22] and praises "heauens power" (5.3.2443) for helping him to prevail over the Black House, even though the victory in fact resulted from the White Knight's superior ability to dissemble.[23] Although these comments fall short of a direct indictment, they also leave the door wide open for an ironic interpretation, a whispered hint that "truth" and "Heaven's power" might in fact be no more than rhetorical constructs that the King manipulates to frame events in his own favor. As Davies and Young suggest—and as at least some spectators at the Globe were clearly ready to believe—the morally ambiguous world presented by Middleton in *Game* stands in stark contrast to the easy, binary worldview projected by the chess allegory and Buckingham's discovery narrative.

The White King's conspicuously slanted notion of truth is entirely consistent with a pattern of characterization that repeatedly invites comparison with criticism in news culture of James's doctrine of absolutism, his lackluster response to the crisis in the Palatinate, and his inability to perceive corruption and dissemblance at court. For another example, consider the hints of incompetence underlying the White King's reaction to the discovery of his traitorous pawn.[24]

> has my Goodnes,
> Clemencie, loue, and fauour gratious raysde thee
> from a Condition next to popular Labour
> took thee from all the dubitable hazards
> of Fortune, her most unsecure aduentures
> and grafted thee into a Branch of honor
> and dost thou fall from the Top-bough by the
> rottenness, of thy alone Corruption, like a Fruite
> thats ouer ripend by the beames of Fauour
>
> (3.1.1369–77)

Shocked at the betrayal of his "clemency, love, and favour," the White King compares the traitorous pawn to a piece of fruit that fell "from the top-bough by the rottenness / Of thy alone corruption" (69–70). Richard Dutton argues that "thy *alone* corruption" excuses James to a certain extent, even though "it is difficult to avoid the reflection that a more vigilant master would have recognized the treachery sooner."[25] He points out that the line "could mean 'your unique corruption' (i.e., no one else was corrupt) or 'your corruption alone' (i.e., there were no other grounds for your fall)," and suggests that "either construction amounts to an implied defense of both the court and the King—the Pawn is to be seen as a unique rotten apple in an otherwise blameless court."[26] Although I agree with Dutton's reading as far it goes, I would add that the staging of the scene makes another, quite different, interpretation very clearly available as well. As the audience knows, the White King's Pawn is not "unique" at all: another "rotten apple," the Fat Bishop, stands among the members of the White House, waiting for an opportune moment to reveal his reversion to the Black side. Like Duncan in *Macbeth*, the White King expresses his shock at the betrayal of a trusted subject while another traitor (or potential traitor) stands under his nose.[27] His obliviousness and poor instincts raise implicit questions about his fitness to rule—precisely the same sort of questions that popular discourse repeatedly raised, more explicitly, in regard to the rule of James I himself.

On a similar note, *Game* also evokes rumors of a sexual relationship between James and the Duke of Buckingham (George Villiers, Middleton's White Duke), formerly one of the most hated and talked-about men in England, but, following the popularity of the discovery narrative, suddenly a hero of the Protestant cause. Like Robert Carr before him, Buckingham was the king's "favorite," a position of preference that brought him a number of peerage positions and eventually made him the most powerful subject outside of the royal family. As Alastair Bellany has shown, the intense closeness between the elderly king and the young, handsome courtier fueled widespread rumors of sexual intimacy: "A number of texts, nearly all dating from the early 1620s, explicitly register suspicions of a homosexual relationship between king and favourite. These suspicions are rich in political implications, especially since they cluster chronologically around the Spanish Match crisis of 1618–23." Bellany argues that fears surrounding the Spanish Match dovetailed with the Buckingham sex rumors because Jacobeans regarded sodomy as "a particularly popish vice . . . the most wicked of sexual transgressions . . . an appropriate expression of the sheer moral degradation of those who had abandoned true religion."[28] This connection goes some way toward explaining the profusion of sodomy references in *Game:* "wee draw / together now for all the world, like 3 Flyes wth / one Strawe thorough theire Buttocks" (3.2.1517–19);[29] "Sodomie, sixpence, you should put that Summe euer / on the Backside of youre Booke, Bishop" (4.2. 1897–98);[30] "they put theire pens the Hebrewe waye mee thinkes" (1.1.437);[31] and so on. In a play about the Spanish Match, these repeated references to sodomy would inevitably remind audiences of James and Buckingham.

Richard Dutton finds strong evidence to support this interpretation in the "bagging" sequence at the end of the play, where the White Duke refers to the Black Duke as "an Oliue-Colourd Ganimed" (5.3.2436), a reference to the myth of the Trojan boy kidnapped by Zeus and forced to serve as cupbearer on Mount Olympus:

> "An olive-coloured Ganymede" is a greenish catamite; "olive-coloured" clearly identifies Olivares [Grand Chamberlain to Philip IV of Spain] as the Black Duke. On the whole, the relationship between Philip IV—a young and new king—and his grand chamberlain would have meant very little to English audiences; besides, the Black Duke is a very minor character in the play, who never speaks more than two lines at a time, and only ever in support. It is therefore rather surprising that he is accorded the prominence of being the last character into the bag. Most striking of all, Olivares was significantly older than his king (37 in 1624 as against Philip's 19), so, whether or not there was anything sexual in their relationship, to dub *him* the "Ganymede" is pointedly inappropriate. It is difficult not to conclude that English audiences were expected to "apply" (laterally) the Jove/Ganymede relationship of the Spanish king and duke to the aging James and his own young duke/favourite.[32]

Dutton's (highly speculative) theory seems particularly correct in light of an anonymous verse libel that portrays James and Buckingham as Jove and Ganymede. In an analysis of the libel, Bellany notes that the Ganymede myth was "in many ways ideally suited to attacks on James's relationship with Buckingham [because] the favourite's first court office had been as royal cupbearer, and the social and age disparity between Jove and Ganymede was replicated in the relationship of king and favourite."[33] This insight into the contemporary resonance of the myth suggests that the White Duke's description of the Black Duke may well be another manifestation of Middleton's delicate irony, a self-implicating statement along the lines of the White King's "thy alone Corruption" line in response to the discovery of his traitorous pawn (3.1.1369–77), or his expression of gratitude to "Heauens power" at the end of the play (5.3.2443). Like these opaque but nevertheless available glances at the king's fitness to rule, the subtle evocation of James's alleged sexual relationship with Buckingham contributes to an understated "graying" of the White House.

Another important, less-than-flattering, glance at the purported "hero" of the discovery narrative arises earlier in the same scene when the White Duke makes a pair of remarks revealing faults attributed to Buckingham in reality.[34] The first of these revelations occurs just after the White Knight responds to the Black Knight's long speech on "white-house Gurmundizers" (5.3.2242) by sardonically remarking that he will "bee halfe afrayde to feede hereafter" (5.3.2263). Comically misapprehending his companion's satirical tone, the White Duke earnestly concurs: "or I beshrewe my heart, for I feare Fatnes / the Fognes of Fatnes, as I feare a Dragon / the Comlines I wish for thats as glorious" (5.3.2264–66). As Elena Levy-Navarro has noted, the White Duke's vain fixation on "comeliness" evokes contemporary resentment over Buckingham's preferment, which derived from James's admiration of his slender, handsome features.[35] A similarly incriminating revelation occurs seventy-three lines later, as the White Knight makes a series of false disclosures in order to trick the Black Knight into revealing the full depravity of the Black House. Comically misapprehending his companion's intended meaning once again, the White Duke makes a disclosure of his own:

> Wh.D. but how shall I bestowe the Vice I bring (Sirs)
> you quite forgett mee, I shall bee lockt out
> by youre strickt Key of life;
> Bl.K$^{t.}$ is yours so fowle (Sir)
> wh.D. some that are pleasde to make a Wanton on't,
> call it infirmitie of bloud, Flesh-Frayltie,
> but certayne theres a worse Name in youre bookes for't.
>
> (5.3.2332–38)

As the Black Knight points out in the proceeding lines, "flesh-frailty" refers to "Venerie" (5.3.2340), or obsessive fixation on sexual pleasure, a condition that humoral theory attributed to an imbalance in the blood. The confession is the most direct reference to Buckingham's reputation for lechery in *Game,* and therefore poses a significant problem for any interpretation that explains the play as an exercise in propaganda or as a straightforward expression of national pride. Attempting to get around the problem, proponents of a "jingoistic" reading have argued that, because the White Duke is speaking within the context of an effort to deceive the Black Knight, his comments should not count as a genuine confession—a defense that fails to appreciate the comic function that the character plays in the scene (the joke, I suggest, is that he does not understand that the White Knight is lying).[36] But to argue over the meaning of the line is to miss the point. The more important observation is that, regardless of whatever assumptions one might infer in regard to the White Duke's intentions, his confession still raises the specter of anticourt discourse. Even though it may not be consistent with other ideas or sentiments suggested elsewhere in the play, such discourse is still on the table, so to speak, and therefore makes a significant contribution to the thinking-through of news culture that Middleton embarks on in *Game.*

The same point also holds for the expositions of White House corruption coming from the Black Knight. Consider, for example, the character's long speech at the beginning of the third act, in which he brags about his ability to influence policy in the White Kingdom:

> the Court ha's held the Cittie by the Hornes
> whilst I haue milkt her; I haue had good soapes too,
> from Countrie Ladies for theire Liberties,
> from some, for theire most uaynelie hopde preferments,
> high offices in the Ayre, I should not liue
> but but for this Mel Aerium, this Mirth-Manna.
>
> (3.1.1174–80)[37]

Following the example of the infamous pamphleteer Thomas Scott, this bragging, confessional speech shows that the Black Knight's power derives from his domestic enablers: the courtiers he has manipulated, the women he has seduced, and the authorities he has bribed. A similar, even more pointed attack occurs in 5.3 (shortly before the White Knight's first confession), when the villain delivers a lengthy speech on the similarity between the feasts at the White court and the gluttony of Roman emperors—comparing the White courtiers, at one point, to "the Hogs / wch Scalliger cites, that could not moue for Fat, / so insensible of eyther Prick or Goade, / that Mice made Holes to Needle in theire buttocks / and they nere felt em (5.3.2243–47). Grotesque comparisons such as these telegraph popular disapproval of courtly excesses, particularly the extravagant feasts hosted by the Duke of Buckingham. Like the White Duke's confession, the attacks carry significant weight, even though they come from a notorious liar and villain, because they make a place for anticourt voices in the overall conversation—buffered and muffled, to be sure, but still a significant element in Middleton's representation of the English court.

To conclude this section, I want to introduce one further, very elegant, example that makes a brilliant comparison between theatrical discourse and the shallowness of the "black versus white" worldview inherent in Buckingham's discovery narrative. The following is from the White Queen's Pawn speech in 5.2., in which she scolds the Black Bishop's Pawn for behaving in a lewd manner while dressed in clerical attire:

> the World's a Stage on wch all parts are playde
> you'de thinke it most absurd to haue a deuill
> presented there not in a Deuills shape,
> or wanting one to send him out in yours,
> you'de rayle at that for an Absurditie
> no Colledge e'er committed, for decorum's sake then,
> for pitties cause, for sacred Vertues honor,
> if you'le persist still in your Deuills part
> present him as you should doo, and let one
> that carries up the goodnes of the playe
> come in that habit, and Ile speake wth him,
> then will the parts bee fitted and the Spectators
> knowe wch is wch, it must be strange cunning
> to finde it else, for such a one as you
> is able to deceiue a mightie Audience,
> naye, those you haue seducst if there bee anie
> in the Assemblie, if they see what manner
> you playe youre Game wth mee, they cannot loue you;
> is there so litle hope of you to smile, Sir;?
>
> (5.2.2076–94)

The Black Bishop's Pawn is smiling because the White Queen's Pawn is hopelessly naive. She longs for a world that operates like morality plays, where devils look like devils and priests look like priests, and spectators do not have to exercise "cunning" judgment to tell the difference. Middleton underlines the simplicity of her viewpoint by inviting comparison with *Game,* a much more sophisticated style of drama where clearcut conventions of signification do not apply. His comparison suggests that, in the real world, "absurdity" in fact derives from an inability to see through false dichotomies such as "hero versus villain," or "black versus white." The witty, metatheatrical exposition of this point implicitly credits addressees with the judgment that the White Queen's Pawn so clearly lacks, thereby contrasting her naïveté with the theatrical public's postulated ability to see beyond the ostensible moral purity of the (not so) White House—and by implication, beyond the purported heroism of Charles and Buckingham.

Hispanophobia and Hispanophilia

The next transposition concerns the popular perception of Spain as an evil empire and the former Spanish ambassador, Gondomar, as a Machiavellian mastermind bent on delivering England into the hands of the Antichrist. Like Buckingham's discovery narrative, this view of England's relation to Spain was the product of long-standing religious tensions and Protestant anxieties over James's foreign policy. It was also a distinctive product of 1620s news culture. As noted, Middleton wrote in a period of rapidly expanding media, a period when the modern conception and social function of news began to come into its own for the very first time. In addition to the growing abundance of ballads, corantos, and various other mechanisms for transmitting information and opinion, the incipient news industry also turned out a steady stream of vehemently anti-Spanish, anti-Catholic polemical pamphlets. This category of literature includes many of the sources Middleton had at hand as he wrote, most notably *The Foot Out of the Snare* (Gee), *The Friers Chronicle* (Goad), *Vox Coeli* (Reynolds), *The Anatomy of the English Nunnery at Lisbon* (Robinson), *Vox Populi* (Scott), and *The Second Part of Vox Populi* (Scott).[38] Texts such as these provided *Game* with an ideologically charged, apocalyptic language that framed England as a vulnerable virgin perpetually threatened by pestiferous, ubiquitous Jesuit arch-seducers working to establish a "universal monarchy." As Howard-Hill has noted, Middleton's most prominent source in this regard was the bestselling author of 1623, Thomas Scott, an evangelical propagandist who "canonized English attitudes to and experience of Gondomar" in a fictionalized portrait that "superseded history in the public awareness."[39] Scott presented himself to readers as "Vox Populi," "the people's voice," a champion of truth and popular consensus in a bitter war between true religion (Protestantism) and the Antichrist (Catholicism).[40] His opposition to the Catholic Church formed the basis for an international policy that promoted alliances with Protestant nations and condemned the influence of any nation associated with Rome, especially the Catholic superpower Spain. In order to avoid casting James as an agent of the Antichrist, Scott generally blamed foreigners at court for the failures he found in official policy. Gondomar's close relationship to James made him an ideal villain, a pariah whom Scott could hold responsible for all of England's problems, including everything from sheep rot to the Spanish Match. In *Vox Populi* (1620), Scott offered readers an insider's perspective on the proceedings of the Spanish council, where Gondomar recounts innumerable plots against England in a series of self-exposing speeches that borrowed quite intentionally from theatrical methods of characterization, another example of a public-making practice that brought the theatrical and print publics closer together.[41] The overall depiction of the Spanish ambassador as a Machiavellian mastermind at the root of every problem in England formed the prototype for Middleton's Black Knight, the primary antagonist in *Game*.

Using the same technique demonstrated in his transposition of the discovery narrative, Middleton reoriented the significance of Scott's Gondomar caricature by bringing it into conversation with contrasting contemporary viewpoints. Recent work on exchanges between Spain and England by Alexander Samson and others has revealed a strong element of Hispanophilia complicating, and coexisting with, the virulent Hispanophobia expressed by the polemical pamphleteers. This vogue for Spanish culture directed tastes in art, fashion, and literature in the years that followed Charles's trip to Madrid. Samson's research shows that the trend had a particularly significant impact on the book trade of 1623:

> Sixteen twenty-three uncovered in London the latent Hispanophilia of a significant sector of the cultural elite, apparent from the existence of an industry of professional language teachers with their competitive publication of textbooks, in the reissue of sumptuous bilingual dictionaries and in the work of professional translators producing Englished versions of the best of Spain's cultural goods. We can also see in 1623 the ongoing popularity of official versions of Spanish, Catholic devotional material. While 1623 may be for us above all the year of the First Folio, for contemporaries the importance and influence of the Hispanic world on English Renaissance culture would never have been in any doubt.[42]

Not surprisingly, the trend became manifest in the theater as well. Annabel Patterson has noted a sudden profusion of "plays with Spanish themes or titles" that began to appear after Charles's return from Spain (85). These works include *The Spanish Gypsy* (Middleton and Rowley; perf. 1623), *The Spanish Viceroy* (sometimes attributed to Phillip Massinger; perf. 1624), and *The Spanish Contract* (author unknown; perf. 1624). By incorporating Spanish style and culture into their productions, Middleton and his colleagues created a populuxe version of an aesthetic experience otherwise beyond the reach of ordinary people, an aesthetic experience people clearly had a desire to engage.[43] Spain may have aroused tremendous fear and hatred in Jacobean England, but it also attracted demonstrable admiration and emulation. Rather than merely propagating the vitriolic anxieties of the pamphleteers, *Game* reflects the complex, diversified attitude of a tiny nation pitted against a fearsome but undeniably fascinating empire.[44]

An appreciation of how *Game* appealed to a fascination with Spanish culture requires close attention to visual detail. As a producer of Lord Mayor's shows and other civic pageants, Middleton acquired substantial expertise in the art of devising theatrical spectacles, an especially prominent feature of later plays such as *Women Beware Women* and *The Changeling*. In *Game*, he treated audiences to a lavish display of contrasting English and Spanish fashions, a striking visual design that accentuated the chess allegory by presenting a clear means for distinguishing between members of the White and Black Houses. Traces of the prominence of Spanish costuming in performance occur throughout the text. Consider, for example, the first entrance of the Black Bishop's Pawn:

> Enter the Bl B.s p.
> a Iesuite
> [Bl.Qs.p.] and here comes hee whose Sanctimonious breath
> can make that Sparke a Flame, list to him, Virgin,
> at whose first Entrance, Princes will fall prostrate,
> weomen are weaker Vessells,
> wh.Q^{s}p. by my pœnitence
> a comlye præsentation, and the habit,
> to admiration reuerend.
>
> (1.1.138–44)

The Black Queen's Pawn aggrandizes the Jesuit's entrance by commanding the White Queen's Pawn to bow, noting that even princes "fall prostrate" before him. The White Queen's Pawn registers her surprise at the Black Bishop's Pawn's appearance with an oath ("By my penitence"), and immediately remarks on his "comely," or pleasing, "presentation." Her choice of the word "habit" indicates that he is likely wearing the black vestments of his order, attire that provokes her "reverend," or respectful, "admiration." This reception offers a clue as to how Middleton expected his audience to react to the Jesuit's entrance. His handsome features and exotic style of dress excite awestruck respect, and no doubt a certain amount of fear as well. The setup for his entrance anticipates the thrill an audience would experience upon seeing their vaunted "enemy" on display before their very eyes.

A similar appeal is notable in the effects for Middleton's spectacular final act, which offers audience members a vivid reimagining of Charles's visit to the Spanish court. The act begins with the entrance of the Black Knight in his litter, the first in a series of theatrical surprises that lead up to the climactic "bagging" scene in 5.3. Shortly after Gondomar's entrance, the Black King enters with his full entourage to greet the White Knight and the White Duke, who enter from the opposite side of the stage (5.1.2012). To formally welcome the visitors to the Black House, the Black Bishop's Pawn delivers a congratulatory oration in Latin. This speech, which the vast majority of theatergoers would have found incomprehensible, signals the travelers' entry into the mysterious, ceremonial world of the Roman Catholic Church (5.1.2017–27). To make the significance of the location absolutely clear, Middleton has the White Knight note in an aside that the atmosphere has "a taste / of the ould Vessell still, the erroneous rellish" (5.1.2036–37), a reference to the so-called old religion and its "erroneous" emphasis on pseudo-miraculous contrivances. As if in response to the White Knight's comment, an altar with statues standing on either side appears in an enclosed space at the back of the stage. As music plays from out of nowhere, a singer performs a song of welcome and commands the illumination of magical candles: "maye from the Altar flames aspire / those Tapors set themselues afire" (5.1.2045–46). At the end of the song, the statues begin to move and dance, an effect derived from Francis Beaumont's *Masque of the Inner Temple and Grayes Inne*.[45] In his notes for this moment in the Revels Series edition, Howard-Hill suggests that a Protestant audience would have "interpreted such manifestations as Catholicism's idolatrous appeal to credulous ignorance. . . . The spectacle was easily arranged in the theatre, but it merely confirmed what the White Knight expected to find in the Black House."[46] This interpretation fails to recognize the undeniably entertaining dimension in Middleton's presentation of derisive Catholic stereotypes. *Game* makes Catholicism look extremely appealing, not just for "credulous" Catholics, but for the Protestants in the audience as well. Nothing in the scene suggests that the invisible music, dancing statues, and self-lighting candles are not actually supernatural within the world of the play. Middleton invited his audience to imagine the reality of these wonders, while simultaneously inviting reflection on the conspicuous theatricality of the Catholic Mass. His version of the Spanish court is a tremendously attractive fantasy designed to engage the contemporary anxieties and fascination surrounding Spain.

Theater as News Event

The final transposition I would like to discuss concerns the popular conversation surrounding *Game* itself and the migration of that conversation from the theater into a variety of new spaces. As noted above, the play had an unprecedented social impact deriving for the most part from the extraordinary popularity generated by the players' direct representation of public men. Although commercial drama had always traded on political comment, it typically avoided direct representation of individuals by removing the action to a distant locale or by disguising personalities behind the gauze of a sophisticated conceit. *Game* took political representation a step further by actually impersonating living public persons, most notably Gondomar, a striking figure who made regular appearances around the city during his long ambassadorship.[47] To make their representation of Gondomar unmistakable, the players went to the trouble of re-creating his distinctively Spanish suit of clothes in precise detail. Depictions of the Black Knight (i.e., Gondomar) on the title pages of the first and third quartos (see figs. 2 and 3) offer some idea of how the character likely appeared on stage: mustachioed with a wide-brimmed hat, a fur-lined cloak, a chain, and large ruffs around his neck and wrists—a blatant imitation of the Gondomar portrait on the title page of Scott's *The Second Part of Vox Populi* (see fig. 1). In addition to Gondomar's elaborate apparel, the players also re-created his famous litter, a well-known sight on the streets of London for many years (see fig. 1).[48] Gondomar required the litter because he suffered from an anal fistula that made transport extremely painful. The vehicle therefore came equipped with a special chair that had a hole cut into the seat to ease discomfort (see fig. 1). Following Scott, Middleton made the fistula an object of unrelenting mockery, a grotesque metonymy for the corruption of the Black House. All of this attention to personalized visual detail had a clear impact on the production's overall appeal: every single contemporary record except one mentions Gondomar, and four refer to the litter specifically.[49] Records also show that some Londoners referred to *Game* simply as "the Play of Gondomar," an alternative title that emphasizes the aspect of the play they found most notable and exciting.[50] By representing actual public figures, Middleton thrilled his audience with the promise of a new opportunity for participation in public life, an opportunity that hinged on their willingness to think of themselves as part of the social entity postulated by theatrical discourse.

It would be a mistake, however, to suppose that the opportunity to see and judge public men was the only element fueling popularity. Contemporary documentation suggests the crowd at the Globe operated something like a friendly riot, a collective expression of enthusiasm that escalated in a spontaneous, organic fashion, growing in size and intensity as it attracted more and more people who simply wanted to share in the excitement. At a certain point, it seems that a significant, if not primary, source of attraction became the crowd itself—*Game*-the-*event* superseded the significance of *Game*-the-*play*. Consider, for example, the report from the Spanish ambassador, Don Carlos Coloma (Gondomar's replacement):

> The actors whom they call here "the King's men" have recently acted, and are still acting, in London a play that so many people come to see, that there were more than 3000 persons there on the day that the audience was smallest. There was such merriment, hubbub and applause that even if I had been many leagues away it would not have been possible for me not to have taken notice of it. . . . All this has been so much applauded and enjoyed by the mob here, where no play has been acted for more than one day, this one has already been acted on four, and each day the crowd is greater.[51]

Coloma's emphasis on the size and noise of the crowd recurs throughout contemporary records. Three other documents note the extraordinary number of people in attendance, and two mention the applause, which Coloma says was audible from "many leagues" away. "Many leagues" is obviously a rough estimate, and probably an exaggeration as well, but even if the noise carried over a radius of a single "league" (which usually referred to a distance of approximately 4.8 kilometers), people would

Fig. 1. Title page for *The Second Part of Vox Populi* showing a portrait of Gondomar with his "chair of ease" and specially constructed litter, a familiar sight on the streets of London. The pamphlet purports to be a transcript of Gondomar's secret meetings, but was in fact written by the anti-Catholic polemicist Thomas Scott, one of the best-selling authors of the 1620s. On a similar note, the pamphlet claims to have been printed in Holland (Goricom)—thereby lending itself a contraband cachet—but was in fact printed in London by Nicholas Okes. STC 22103.2. By permission of the Folger Shakespeare Library.

Fig. 2. Title page of *A Game at Chess,* Quarto 3, showing a portrait of the Black Knight (Gondomar) passing a secret letter "from his holiness" to the Fat Bishop (Marco Antonio Dominis). The portrait of the Black Knight bears a significant (and presumably purposeful) resemblance to the portrait of Gondomar on the cover of Thomas Scott's *The Second Part of Vox Populi* (see fig. 1). In a further resemblance, the quarto claims to have been printed in Holland (Ghedruckt in Lydden), but was in fact printed in London—probably by Ian Masse. In the background, there is an image of "the bag," or Hellmouth, that suggests what the property may have looked like onstage. STC 17884. By permission of the Folger Shakespeare Library.

Fig. 3. Title page of *A Game at Chess,* Quarto 1, suggesting what the costumes for the Fat Bishop, Black Duke, Black Queen, Black King, White King, White Queen, White Duke, and White Bishop may have looked like in performance. As is the case with the title page for Quarto 3 (see fig. 2), the portrait of the Black Knight bears an unmistakable similarity to the portrait of Gondomar on the cover of Thomas Scott's *The Second Part of Vox Populi* (see fig. 1). STC 17882.2. By permission of the Folger Shakespeare Library.

have heard it throughout most of London. *Game*-the-play spoke to an audience of thousands, but *Game*-the-event spoke to an entire city.

In addition to the personation of Gondomar, the crowds, and the applause, contemporary records also repeatedly mention profit and imminent conflict with the authorities, elements that played a key role in shaping the way Londoners understood the excitement surrounding *Game:*

> "Each time they have performed it the players have taken in 300 gold scudos. . . . It is believed nevertheless that it will be prohibited once the King has notice of it."[52]
>
> "The players have gotten 100li the day euer since, for they play no thing els, knowing there time cannot be long."[53]
>
> "Had so much ben donne the last yeare, they had eueryman ben hanged for it."[54]
>
> "But the Players looseth no tyme, nor forbeareth to make haye while the Sunn shyneth."[55]

As a close observer of the social scene, Middleton quickly recognized that the unexpected reversal of James's Spanish policy opened up new possibilities for theatrical representation—and profit. In 1624, the impersonation of public figures *seemed* much riskier than it actually was (Dutton 53–54).[56] Only four years earlier, with negotiations for a Spanish match in full swing, James I had issued a declaration warning his subjects that "matters of state . . . are no Theames, or subjects fit for vulgar persons or common meetings," so all citizens "from the highest to the lowest," should "take heede, how they intermeddle by Penne, or Speech, with causes of State, and secrets of Empire" (Larkin 496).[57] *Game* marketed itself as a direct challenge to such restrictions, blatantly inviting "vulgar persons" to "intermeddle" on an imaginative basis. This tactic had the side effect of making actual public participation seem possible, not only for theatergoers, but also for English society at large, for anyone who heard news that the "Play of Gondomar" existed. Historical records suggest the players' gambit paid off handsomely. Authorities shut the play down after nine days, most likely for reasons of diplomatic decorum, but in that time it generated profits estimated at £1,500—a massive fortune.[58] The company also had to appear before an official review, but this does not seem to have led to serious repercussions: a new production appeared at the Globe a few weeks later, with all players' necks intact.[59] Nevertheless, popular discussion held that the players began performing *Game* on a daily basis because they knew they had gone too far and wanted to capitalize on the notoriety they had generated before authorities intervened. Regardless of whether this rumor was true or not, it served an important function from a public-making perspective because it established a framework that shaped the way people understood the commotion at the Globe. Audiences at *Game* viewed themselves as part of an unfolding narrative, a grand lark that had all the basic elements of a typical Jacobean city comedy: illicit activity, an urban setting, witty protagonists, an impudent ploy, the imminent threat of discovery, and a chance to attain an outrageous fortune. In addition to fulfilling an essential function in the underlying narrative, profit also operated alongside applause and attendance as a quantifiable indicator of popularity. The implicit message running through the repeated enumerations of attendance, audibility, and money collected at the door was that people acted of their own accord, voluntarily participating in a unique expression of collective interest.

In his letter to Dudley Carleton of 21 August, John Chamberlain describes another important characteristic of *Game*-the-event that helps to bring the public created by the theater into greater focus: diversity.

> I doubt not but you haue heard of our famous play of Gondomar, which has ben followed with extraordinarie concourse, and frequented by all sorts of people old and younge, rich and poore, masters and seruants, papists and puritans, wise men et[c] churchmen and statesmen as *sir* Henry wotton, *Sir* Albert morton, *Sir* Benjamin Ruddier, *Sir* Thomas Lake, and a world beside; the Lady Smith wold haue gone yf she could haue persuaded me to go with her, I am not so sore nor seuere but that I would willingly haue attended her, but I could no sit so long, for we must haue ben there before one a'clocke at farthest to find any roome.[60]

As noted above, the early modern theater depended on precisely the type of diversity Chamberlain describes in order to remain commercially viable, and this mandate had a direct effect on how it addressed adherents. His description also underlines the relationship between diversity and other, less structured, forms of discourse caught up in the process of theatrical public making. People went to the theater because they wanted to see and hear the actors onstage, but also because they wanted to see and hear each other, to participate in an intensely physical, synergetic forum for exhibition. In addition to offering people a sense of closeness to nobility, theatrical value also involved a chance to see and be seen by people from all walks of life, "old and younge, rich and poore, masters and seruants, papists and puritans, wise men et[c] churchmen and statesmen."[61] This visceral intensity—the noise and spectacle of people, the dense concentration of bodies acting in relation to each other—constitutes an important distinction between the print public Middleton built on and the theatrical public he helped to create. As a fundamental function of the medium, discourse in the theater involved robust physical interaction: people seeing, hearing, and reacting to each other, making choices about how to appear before each other, and collectively defining a corporate identity that evolved in real time. Unlike a print public, which brings people together by inviting them to *imagine* commonality with a group of remote, mostly unknowable strangers, the theater made a public where a sense of commonality grew out of physical proximity, and where discourse operated on multiple fields of exchange. Performance, fashion, and applause—not to mention printed playtexts—all played a significant role in the space for conversation that the theater fostered among a rich diversity of adherents.

Ben Jonson's *The Staple of News* provides an evocative final example of how the conversation surrounding *Game* evolved as it forged an increasingly extensive, interconnected discursive space. In a subplot that parodies innovations in the printing industry, Jonson presents an early modern news bureau, or "staple," a fashionable office where agents channel dubious reports from around the world and retail them to credulous Londoners. The frenetic atmosphere of the Staple provides an ideal platform for the rapid-fire satiric exposition of a number of prominent trends in news culture. For example, at 3.2.20, a news agent named Thomas announces that "the King of Spain is chosen Pope," a report that mocks the tendency of anti-Catholic polemicists such as Scott to conflate Spain, Rome, and the Antichrist for rhetorical effect. When asked for news of Gondomar later in the same scene, Thomas reports that the former ambassador has given himself "A second fistula" by using "the poor English play [that] was writ of him" (i.e., *Game*) for the purpose "Of cleansing his posteriors" (3.2.208–10). Jonson's not-so-gentle attack on an extraordinarily successful play from a rival dramatist shows him making a new perspective on *Game* available to new people in a new space, thereby continuing the ongoing process of making the theatrical public. Notably, the reference also carries an implied history of the various manifestations of *Game* that became available in the course of a series of public-making actions: *Game*-the-performance, *Game*-the-event, *Game*-the-quarto, *Game*-the-news-story, and so on. Jonson simultaneously documents, and extends, an ongoing process of publication.

Game involved a series of transpositions *into* and *out of* the theater that collectively exemplify the character and evolution of the early modern theatrical public. Middleton brought together disparate elements from news culture—national pride, religious tension, polemical stereotype, court gossip, Hispanophobia, Hispanophilia, and so on—and integrated them into an artwork that expanded their interpretive potential and generated a conversation that reverberated throughout a wide variety of spaces. The play was exceptional in terms of personation and popularity, but entirely typical in terms of style of address: it appealed to, and also fostered, the critical judgment of a diverse, discerning audience. This observation explains why it is difficult to agree with any reading that interprets the play as a vehicle for ideological indoctrination. As is the case for the best drama of the period in general, meaning in *Game* arises from robust multivocality—not from a straightforwardly expressed message or attitude. Significantly, however, the absence of a unitary political import did not preclude the possibility of substantive political effect. *Game* contributed toward the transformation of the political landscape, and to the idea of news, by cultivating a space where playful, intellectually and emotionally robust thinking about the news could occur.

CHAPTER 4

The Staple of News and the Invention of Media Criticism

No study of theater and news in early modernity could be complete without paying due consideration to Ben Jonson's *The Staple of News* (perf. 1626, pub. 1631), an extraordinary meditation on the social dynamics of news culture that stands as one of the earliest and most thoughtful examples of seventeenth-century media criticism. More than any other play of the era, *Staple* shows the theater actively caught up in a robust process of thinking about news—thereby providing news culture with a space where it could develop the reflexive, critical dimension fundamental to the new idea of news that began to coalesce in the period. In a critical analysis of the exploitation and abuse of specialized terminologies, news becomes the primary example of what Jonson saw as the generally degraded quality of social discourse, a problem he connects to the commodification of knowledge and the increasing participation of society at large in public conversation. Underlying this very vigorous critique, however, there is also a positive claim for poetry as a superior mode for knowing the world and a corresponding claim for theater as a superior platform for informed public commentary. Asserting the same categorical difference between drama and news that Shakespeare developed in *The Winter's Tale,* he thus moves to bolster the value of his own art by denigrating a (putatively) competing discursive form. As noted in regard to *The Winter's Tale,* however, his process of drawing a contrast between the two forms also involves a self-conscious acknowledgment of common ground—an awareness that, for better or worse, drama and news were complicit in, and dependent on, an escalation in opportunities for participation in public life and the new ways of thinking that came along with it.

Jonson and News

Staple gave full dramatic treatment to ideas about news that Jonson had been working on, in various ways, for most of his career.[1] For the most part, these ideas cohere with the popular attitude (discussed in the foregoing chapters) that regarded news as an overgrown form of gossip—a silly, fashionable luxury sold by unscrupulous vendors to credulous, voracious consumers. In *Epicœne* (1609), for example, True-wit warns the elderly gentleman Morose against taking a much younger bride by suggesting that she will spend all of his money on luxuries such as jewels, silverware, velvets, and news ("what was done at Salisbury, what at the Bath, what at court, what in progress," 2.2.99–100), and the argument for *The Alchemist* (1610) lists news among the bogus whimsies proffered by the con men who have set up shop in Lovewit's vacated London home ("Much company they draw, and much abuse / In casting figures, telling fortunes, news," 10–11).[2] As the quote from *The Alchemist* demonstrates, Jonson identified news with individuals at the margins of society, figures, such as Shakespeare's Autolycus, who combined selling with stealing and fraud. The most prominent example in this regard is the balladeer Nightingale from *Bartholomew Fair* (1614), who advertises titles of mock ballads on the same basic model as the "singing fish ballad" and "moneybag ballad" from *The Winter's Tale* 4.4 ("What is't you buy? '*The Windmill blown down by the Witch's Fart!*'" 2.4.19).[3] Later on in the play, we discover that the balladeer's primary source of income is in fact theft: he works in cooperation with the pickpocket Edgeworth, who robs the distracted customer Cokes, a credulous, rustic consumer serving the same dramatic function (the dupe) as Mopsa, Dorcas, and the Shepherd's son (3.5.1–180).

For the most part, however, Jonson's figures of consumer credulity are not wide-eyed rural innocents, but half-witted, urban obsessives—the so-called newsmongers known for their addiction to semiprivate news forms such as manuscript newsletters and the reports circulated orally among acquaintances at St. Paul's.[4] The most prominent manifestation of this type in the dramatist's earlier work is Sir Politic Would-be from *Volpone* (1606), a news-loving, English tourist in Venice whose very name betokens a misplaced trust in the intellectual value of following the news (he wants to be, but isn't, "politic," or wise). In an early scene with Peregrine (a more sagacious fellow traveler), Would-be attempts to present himself as a sophisticated political insider, but comes off as a gullible buffoon when he asks for confirmation in regard to a story about a raven that has purportedly built a nest in one of the king's ships (2.1.18–22).[5] Immediately recognizing that the story is nothing more than superstitious nonsense, Peregrine initiates a discussion of contemporary news events that becomes increasingly absurd as it goes along. The exchange is an important touchstone for the present study because it shows Jonson developing a satiric technique that he would employ on a much larger scale some twenty years later in *Staple*—a technique that focuses derision, not only on the subject matter of news discourse, but also on the gaudy, exotic style of rhetoric that it offered in place of actual substance.

Musing over the portent of the ominous raven's nest, the travelers discuss a series of similar stories all falling into the general category of "prodigy tales":[6] a lioness has given birth to "another whelp" in the Tower of London (a reference to an actual lion who gave birth to her second cub in the tower on 26 February 1605) (2.1.34–35), "fires" have appeared in the sky at Berick (a reference to reports of luminous phenomenon, perhaps the aurora borealis, from 7 December 1604) (2.1.36), astronomers have discovered a "new star" (a reference to a supernova that appeared on 30 September 1604) (2.1.37), and a number of creatures—including six porpoises and a whale—have appeared in the Thames past the London Bridge (a reference to the capture of a single porpoise—not six—at West Ham on 19 January 1606 and the sighting of a whale in the Thames in January 1606) (2.1.40–48). The whale story initiates a shift from prodigies to news of international events: Would-be immediately concludes that the animal was "either sent from Spain, or the Archdukes! / Spinola's whale, upon my life" (a reference to two of the most commonly invoked pariahs in foreign news: the Cardinal Archduke Albert of Austria, ruler of the Spanish Netherlands, and Ambrogio de Spinola, commander of the Spanish army in the Netherlands) (2.1.50–51).[7] A similar response follows a report on the death of Mas Stone, a drunken illiterate who Would-be claims was a master spy responsible for transmitting secret messages between England and the Low Countries (2.1.67–74).[8] Hoping to somehow overwhelm the newsmonger's credulity, Peregrine finally invents a blatantly false story about a gang of baboon spies from a "nation near China" (2.1.88–89). To his amazement, however, Would-be replies that he has knowledge of the gang, and, adopting a pedantic tone, authoritatively refers to them as "the Mameluchi" (the name of an Egyptian dynasty bearing no connection whatsoever to either baboons or China) (2.1.90).

By emphasizing the exotic, secretive dimension of his parodic news reports, Jonson indexes the newsmonger's elitist self-image and ignorant preference for style over substance. Although certain elements, such as prodigy narratives, were common in all commercially printed forms, it is clear, from various references throughout the play, that the particular object of Would-be's obsession is the privately circulated newsletter.[9] As noted above, he luxuriates in the strange language and pseudo-confidentiality of putatively secret news because it gives him a false sense of exclusive knowledge, a claim to superiority based on a fantasy of special access to the inner workings of world affairs. This pride in exclusivity helps to explain the horror he expresses at the end of the play, when he removes his tortoise-shell disguise and realizes that he has been the victim of a humiliating hoax: "O, I shall be the fable of all feasts, / the freight of the gazette, ship-boys tale; / And, which is worst, talk for ordinaries" (5.5.83–85).[10] For Would-be, a vain connoisseur of private news, the most painful part of the hoax is not the immediate humiliation of the event itself, but the thought that news of the event will circulate in nonexclusive, public forums, thereby becoming a fable at "feasts," a report in commercial news products ("the freight of the gazette"[11]), gossip for sailors, and, worst of all, the subject of everyday conversation at inns ("ordinaries"). In short, the fate he imagines amounts to a hell made especially for newsmongers: unlimited exposure to the open, common talk that privileged news discourse defined itself against.

Although Jonson's nondramatic writings relate less directly to my central argument, it is still worth noting that his attitude toward news culture also finds expression throughout a number of poems. In *The New Cry* (1616), for example, he derides the fashionable, ruff- and cuff-adorned newsmongers who converse obsessively about the latest foreign reports from "the Gazetti or *Gallo-Belgicus*" (l. 16) and exchange secret messages written "with juice of lemons, onions, [and] piss" (l. 28), but are nevertheless "wrong" (l. 40) in all of their opinions and utterly devoid of substantive knowledge.[12] On a similar note, *An Epistle Answering to one that Asked to be Sealed of the Tribe of Ben* (1623) develops a comparison between "Men that are safe and sure in all they do" (l. 1) and "those that merely talk and never think": lechers, libelers, and gossipers who congregate at inns to discuss the latest news stories over long, drunken meals (an image of extravagant consumption and news that adumbrates the scenes at the

Devil Tavern in *Staple,* act 4). In addition to this grotesque portrait of newsmongering, the poem is also noteworthy for multiple topical references to the news discourse of 1623, especially Prince Charles's momentous trip to Spain. Although he seems conspicuously well informed on the subject, Jonson professes indifference, announcing a preference to leave such matters to the more sagacious judgment of James I: "Whether the dispensation yet be sent / Or that the match from Spain was ever meant? / I wish all well, and pray high heaven conspire / My prince's safety, and my king's desire" (35–38). The same indifference is also manifest in *An Execration Upon Vulcan* (1623), a poem that bemoans the fire (Vulcan) that destroyed Jonson's literary labors and lists, in order of ascending quality, other items he deems more worthy of destruction, beginning with the Talmud and ending with "The weekly Courants [corantos] with Paul's seal, and all / Th'admired discourses of the prophet Ball" (Ball was a lunatic conspiracist who predicted that James I would become pope) (65–84). This bibliographical hierarchy, with Jonson's own works at the very top and news next to the bottom, perfectly encapsulates the same basic attitude articulated in the poems and plays: news is a specious, deficient form of knowledge, utterly inferior to the art of true poets and incapable of supporting serious social discourse.

Of all Jonson's works, none makes the case for poetry over news more directly and forcefully than *News from the New World Discovered in the Moon* (1620), a full-blown attack on news culture that introduced many of the ideas that are developed in *Staple,* including the notion of a news "Staple" (or monopoly) itself.[13] Adopting the same satiric technique employed in the conversation between Sir Politic Would-be and Peregrine from *Volpone* 2.1, the masque opens with an exchange that pits two Heralds (the representatives of poetry) against a Factor, a Printer, and a Chronicler (the representatives of manuscript news, printed news, and history).[14] Jonson gets straight to the heart of his critique in the opening lines:

> FIRST HERALD. News, news, news!
> SECOND HERALD. Bold, and brave news!
> FIRST HERALD. New as the night they are born in—
> SECOND HERALD. Or the fant'sy that begot 'em.
> FIRST HERALD. Excellent news!
> SECOND HERALD. Will you hear any news?
> PRINTER. Yes, and thank you too, sir. What's the price of 'em?
> FIRST HERALD. Price, coxcomb? What price but the price o your ears? As if any man used to pay for anything here!

SECOND HERALD. Come forward. You should be some dull tradesman by your pig-headed sconce now, that think there's nothing good anywhere but what's to be sold.

PRINTER. Indeed, I am all for sale, gentlemen, you say true. I am a printer, and a printer of news, and I do hearken after 'em, wherever they be at any rates. I'll give anything for a good copy now, be't true or false, so't be news. (ll. 1–19)

When the First Herald asks, "What price but the price o your ears?" he implies that the news is free for anybody who wants to hear it—a normative fact of everyday communicative practice that, from his perspective, is obvious and therefore goes without saying. In addition to aligning the character with a more traditional attitude toward the transmission of information, the line directs attention to the main source of Jonson's dissatisfaction with commercial news culture: the commodification of information. The Herald's unfamiliarity with the notion of monetized communication stems from a conception of news as a form of friendly conversation, discourse shared orally and personally among members of a community, primarily for purposes of mutual benefit and without any sort of profit motive. On this view, asking about the price of news is commensurate with asking about the price of familial love or friendship—it imposes a crass, commercial framework on a form of exchange that ought to derive impetus from a basic desire to commune with others. The Printer is thus a "dull tradesman," a witless, lower-class slob unable to appreciate the distinction between true knowledge and nonsense because his value system assesses all information in strictly monetary terms. Unembarrassed by his lack of refinement, the Printer responds by proclaiming an "all for sale" attitude—a willingness to sell any sort of information he can acquire, regardless of truthfulness, and without any concern for the quality of content. Echoing this frank declaration of cynicism, the Chronicler explains how he stretches out the length of his "great book" by recording and repeating trivialities such as the number of lighted candles in a room, thereby fulfilling a contractual obligation to fill up three reams of paper—for him, the value of information inheres solely in the ability of text to fill pages (l. 23). Rounding out the introductions with a third admission, the Factor boasts about the vast network of correspondents he maintains, not only for purposes of profit, but also to foster a reputation among elites. As is the case with the Printer and the Chronicler, his comments disclose a narrow focus on quantity and a cynical indifference to substance: he trades in "puritan news," "protestant news," and "pontifical news," completely unbothered by concerns for confessional allegiance (ll. 36–37). In the centuries that followed, this affectation of neutrality would become a standard mechanism for projecting fairness and authority in news discourse, but it was more suspect in the early seventeenth century, as the Factor's blithe comments suggest, because it indicated a fundamental lack of conviction—an equivocating reluctance to take sides. When he returned to the same material a few years later in *Staple,* Jonson would develop this angle of critique in fuller dramatic detail by having the "pontifical" and "protestant" reporters switch portfolios at a moment's notice to placate the whim of their wealthy benefactor.

Toward the end of his self-introduction, the Factor makes a point of putting distance between himself and the Printer, noting his ambition to create a centralized "staple for news" that will provide manuscript newsletters to exclusive customers under a single brand, thereby offering a more authentic-seeming alternative to the "conundrums" currently available in print. As an example of what he means by "conundrum," he cites a report of "the serpent in Sussex," and a report of "the witches bidding the devil to dinner at Derby," stories that evoke the miracles and monsters that were ubiquitous in the news pamphlets and ballads of the time (ll. 39–44). These comments initiate an exchange that showcases Jonson's acute grasp of how the idea of news had changed over the course of the first few decades of the seventeenth century:

> PRINTER. Sir, that's all one, they were made for the common people, and why should not they ha' their pleasure in believing of lies are made for them, as you have in Paul's that make 'em for yourselves?
>
> FIRST HERALD. There he speaks reason to you, sir.
>
> FACTOR. I confess it, but it is the printing I am offended at. I would have no news printed, for when they are printed they leave to be news. While they are written, though they be false, they remain news still.
>
> PRINTER. See men's diverse opinions! It is the printing of 'em makes 'em news to a great many, who will indeed believe nothing but what's in print. For those I do keep my presses and so many pens going to bring forth wholesome relations, which once in half a score years (as the age grows forgetful) I print over again with a new date, and they are of excellent use. (ll. 45–56)[15]

Pushing back against the Factor's claims to superiority, the Printer acknowledges the absurdity of his stories, but asks where the harm is in providing people with pleasurable lies. The only distinction between the Factor's practice and his own, he argues, is that he produces printed lies for "the common people," whereas the Factor produces manuscript lies for the fashionable newsmongers who congregate at St. Paul's. The Factor responds, not by asserting the greater truthfulness of his reports (as one might expect), but by putting issues of truth to the side—his central objection to print, he says, is that it disseminates news reports to a public audience, thereby depleting the freshness and fashionability that makes information "news" in the first place: "I would have no news printed, for when they are printed they leave to be news. While they are written, though they be false, they remain news still." In effect, he gives voice to an older, elitist view of news characterized by a preoccupation with exclusivity, a view that only regards a report as "news" insofar as it remains within a restrictive social circle. The Printer counters this complaint by remarking on the stark contrast between the Factor's notion of news and the notion held by his own discursive community, which regards the printed status of a text as a token of truthfulness. Pressing the contrast even further, he notes that many of his customers "indeed believe nothing but what's in print"—a line that recalls Mopsa from *The Winter's Tale* 4.4: "I love a ballad in print, a-life, for then we are sure they are true" (ll. 260–61).[16] On balance, the exchange characterizes printed news and manuscript news as more-or-less commensurate vehicles for the same bad idea. Jonson wants to show that, despite their aesthetic and demographic dissimilarities, both forms are essentially degenerate—equally exploitative, equally cynical, and equally insubstantial.

As noted, the masque contrasts the vagaries of news with poetry, a form it upholds as a vastly superior alternative to the products purveyed by the three newsmen. In a series of reports following the Factor's argument with the Printer, the Heralds describe a new world recently discovered "in the orb of the moon" (l.105), thereby developing something like a science fiction satire of Jacobean society. Following the example of the mock news stories in *Volpone* 2.1, these reports combine absurdity with exotic language and topical references, a technique that enables a simultaneous exposure of the speciousness of news and the credulity of its consumers. For example, in an attack on the discord and tumult of the courts, the Second Herald reports that, rather than speech, moon-dwellers employ a harmonious form of discourse that resembles music, thus rendering the lawyers "all dumb as fishes, for they have no controversies to exercise themselves in" (ll. 161–62). On a similar note, the First Herald targets the rising incidence of female transvestitism in Jacobean society with a mock report of a lunar island where "under one article both kinds are signified; for they are fashioned alike, male and female the same, not-heads and broad hats, short doublets, and long points; neither do they ever untruss for distinction, but laugh and lie down in moonshine, and stab with their poniards" (ll. 225–28). In the final lines of the masque, Jonson reveals these fanciful stories for what they truly are—poetry—thereby imbuing them with a significance that posits a stark contrast to the meaningless vapidity of news. Stepping forward to address the King directly, the Second Herald announces that, despite its title, the production has deliberately provided "no news" at all because its purpose is to stimulate "delight," as opposed to mere "belief" (ll. 244–45). This bold revelation returns focus, once again, to an aspect of theatrical discourse that made it an especially effective form for thinking about the representation of current events: unlike news, drama did not attempt to instill addressees with an impression of factuality, or what Jonson refers to in the foregoing quotation as "belief." As *News from the New World* both demonstrates and declares, the players were oriented toward a much loftier response—"delight"—an aim that enabled them to work outside of the narrow constraints of news discourse, allowing for a much fuller, more thoughtful, intellectual and emotional experience.[17]

The Apostrophized Public

I want to begin my analysis of *The Staple of News* proper with a discussion of a metatheatrical mechanism I shall refer to as the "parenthetical hello"—an implicit acknowledgment of the audience that puts them into a feedback loop with the events enacted on stage. To take a well-known example of this mechanism in action, consider "Pyramus and Thisby," the uproarious play-within-a-play from the final act of *A Midsummer Night's Dream.* While Theseus and the lovers watch, Bottom and the mechanicals perform, thereby creating a performance space within the performance space itself. Shakespeare's witty scenographic arrangement has a ticklish, recursive effect akin to the experience of viewing a reflection of one's own reflection or hearing one's own voice rebroadcast at a slight delay. Like a person who looks at himself looking or speaks as he hears himself speaking, the spectators find themselves confronted by an unexpected image of their own activity: they are watching a representation of spectators watching a representation. Of course, the key difference in the case of "Pyramus and Thisby" is that the moment of reflexivity does not happen by chance, but on purpose—someone has designed it, and a realization of the design is part of the surprise. The effect opens up a backchannel of communication, a covert level of meaning that adds a sense of self-awareness, or double consciousness, to the overall production. As the act of spectatorship folds back into the field of representation, we become aware that our encounter with the events on stage is a dialogic exchange—not a one-sided, passive act of observation. Without resorting to overt address, the production is acknowledging our presence. By gesturing from the margins, someone is saying (hello).

The reflexivity I am describing played a key role in the public-making practice of the early modern theater and is a particularly prominent aspect of the media analysis in *The Staple of News*—a play that features four meta-audience members who offer pointedly absurd commentary from the periphery of the stage, thereby confronting the actual audience with an ironic reverse-image of a proposed norm. As noted in chapter 1, formulations such as Jonson's helped to define the theatrical public in relation to older styles of drama and other publics, including the public created by news. To understand how this process of definition functioned, it is helpful to recall Warner's observation, also noted in chapter 1, on the role of reflexivity in public address: all public discourse postulates, and *characterizes,* an active, ongoing space of conversation by praising, contradicting, quoting, scolding, mocking, or otherwise representing the discourse of notional participants purportedly active in a virtual field of exchange. In addition to incorporating other forms of public address, such as competing newspapers or plays, the projected murmur of ongoing conversation might also include the responses of consumers, or other individual adherents attending to the same focus of attention. Warner notes that the *Spectator* made representation of individual participants a standard feature of periodicals in the eighteenth century, anticipating a wide variety of mechanisms—such as "viewer mail, call-in shows, 900-number polling, home video shows, game show contestants, town meetings, studio audiences, and man-on-the-street interviews"—that enable mass media "to characterize their own space of consumption." This process of reflexive representation, or what Warner refers to as a "feedback loop," provides a framework for understanding the (hello) that Jonson issues as he analyses the public dimension of theatrical culture and news culture in *The Staple of News.*[18]

As the play begins, four elderly matrons ("Gossips") interrupt the

Prologue and demand places in the prestigious viewing area on stage, an especially expensive, prominent spot reserved for courtiers or other patrons of distinction. Thus installed, they commence a critical discussion that continues throughout four short "Intermeans" between acts. Despite a blunt delivery, their commentary exhibits a sharp, ironic edge—a salient tension between ostensible and subtextual meaning. As I noted above in regard to metatheatrical formulations, such effects naturally pick up an accent of intentionality when they become manifest in a dramatic context because, for the most part, irony arises in the theater by design, not by chance. Thus, in the process of acknowledging the discord between the Gossips' speech and decorum, we become aware of another parenthetical channel of meaning. Consider how this pattern unfolds during the course of the metatheatrical interruption at the beginning of the play:

> PROLOGUE. For your own sake, not ours—
>
> MIRTH. Come, gossip, be not ashamed. The play is *The Staple of News*, and you are the mistress and lady of Tattle; let's ha' your opinion of it. Do you hear gentleman? What are you, gentleman-usher to the play? Pray you, help us to some stools here.
>
> PROLOGUE. Where? O'the stage, ladies?
>
> MIRTH. Yes, o'the stage. We are persons of quality, I assure you, and women of fashion, and come to see and to be seen: my gossip Tattle here, and gossip Expectation, and my gossip Censure; and I am Mirth, the daughter of Christmas and spirit of Shrovetide. They say "It's merry when gossips meet." I hope your play will be a merry one.
>
> PROLOGUE. Or you will make it such, ladies. Bring a form here. [*A bench is brought. They sit.*] But what will the noblemen think, or the grave wits here, to see you seated on the bench thus? (Induction ll. 1–17)

On an ostensible level, Mirth's description of herself and her companions as "persons of quality" seems reasonably truthful. As far as we can tell, she believes that what she is saying is correct, and she honestly expects the Prologue to accept her claim at face value. At the level of subtext, however, we get a markedly different message. The Gossips' appearance, behavior, and (most of all) gender all offer testimony that comes into sharp contrast with their pretension to exalted social status. Our sense of this contrast becomes particularly acute under the Prologue's direction: he expresses shock ("Where? O'the stage, ladies?"), slyly quips that, even if the play isn't "merry," the Gossips' presence will "make it such," and straightforwardly asks the ladies to consider the impression their appearance on stage might make on the "noblemen" and "grave wits" in the assembly. All of these subtle pointers help to guide our awareness of the ironic tension underlying the Gossips' discussion. As this awareness increases, we move closer and closer toward an inevitable conclusion: Mirth and her companions are absurd.

In this case, however, the absurdity has a nuance that sets it apart from the Mechanicals' metatheatrical performance in *A Midsummer Night's Dream.* As D. F. McKenzie notes in an important essay from 1972, the Gossips' commentary in the first intermean reveals an unexpected depth of knowledge and expertise that complicate the ironic accentuation: they correctly identify the play's genre, themes, allegorical pattern, key symbols, and so on, and display an encyclopedic grasp of theatrical history that goes back more than twenty years.[19] This critical acuity is particularly notable in Mistress Mirth, a character McKenzie describes as a "dramatic theorist, literary historian, and sharp reviewer" strategically positioned at the vanguard of critical response. "Mirth has forestalled most critics," McKenzie writes. "Jonson's projection of his audience of learned owls, wide-eyed but blind, is clearly not just a matter of having a bunch of women of fashion climb on to a stage to give their opinions. It is also a remarkably accurate forecast of subsequent interpretive comment and critical judgment."[20] Although I find this reading generally persuasive, I want to point out that acknowledgment of the Gossips' acumen does not make the irony any less apparent or available. Rather, their intelligence effectively delimits our sense of absurdity, giving the comic derision a more distinct focus: Jonson offers us license to laugh at the Gossips *despite* the strength of their analysis. They are absurd, not because they misunderstand the play, but because they are blind to theatrical standards of taste and decorum, knowledge and experience notwithstanding.

To appreciate the social dynamics underlying this distinction, it is important to note that the Gossip scenes take place in the Blackfriars, a private, indoor theater situated in central London. This location makes a significant difference because, unlike the big, open-air amphitheaters in the unsavory periphery of the city, the private theaters catered to a select audience of scholars and men of fashion—the "noblemen" and "grave wits" that the Prologue refers to in the induction (ll. 15–16). Despite their long theatergoing experience, the Gossips are quite out of place at the Blackfriars, and it shows.[21] For example, Gossip Tattle starts in fear when the Tiremen enter with a torch to light the candles, presumably because this is the first time she has attended a production indoors. Quick to exploit the moment for comic effect, the Prologue mockingly assures her that the Tiremen "carry no fireworks to fright you," an insinuation, as Anthony Parr has noted, that she expects the "vulgar practices of the popular stage."[22] This orientation toward "vulgar" entertainment is the specific focus of Jonson's ironic design: in addition to characterizing the Gossips' behavior, it has an obvious influence on their tastes and opinions. For example, consider Tattle's dissatisfaction with the actors' costumes (1.Int.10–12), her complaint that the play has neither a devil nor a fool (1.Int.20–40), and her stated preference for Vices that brandish wooden daggers (2.Int.10–13). All of these comments highlight the gaudiness of the Gossips' taste, thereby projecting an ironic reverse image of a proposed standard. In short, the metatheatrical chorus effectively personifies the sort of opinions a refined theatergoer ought to define himself *against.*

Significantly, the ironic tension also extends to the Gossips' taste in news—thus bringing the metatheatrical framing device into connection with the play's central thematic concern. For example, consider the following excerpt from the third intermean, wherein the Gossips offer their thoughts on the succession of increasingly ridiculous news reports in 3.2:

> CENSURE. O, they are monstrous! Scurvy and stale! And too exotic; ill cooked and ill dished!
>
> EXCEPTION. They were as good yet as Butter could make them.
>
> TATTLE. In a word, they were beastly buttered! He shall never come o'my bread more, nor in my mouth, if I can help it. I have had better news from the bake-house by ten thousand parts, in a morning, or the conduits in Westminster; all the news of Tuttle Street, and both the Alm'ries, the two Sanctuaries, long and round Woolstaple, with King's Street and Cannon Row to boot. (3.Int.14–23)

The Gossips' continuing play on the word "Butter" refers to Nathaniel Butter, a well-known London printer who published more than four hundred other news documents in the 1620s. As Stuart Sherman has noted, Butter's name, "endlessly metamorphosed," provides fodder for a running joke that recurs throughout the entire play.[23] More significantly, it also contributes to a sustained food analogy that Jonson uses to accentuate the ephemeral, vacuous nature of various news forms. Notably, however, the Gossips' dissatisfaction with the news in the play focuses, not so much on substance—which is Jonson's primary concern—but on style: it is "too exotic," "ill dished," and "beastly buttered." Rather than the reports of foreign wars and political maneuverings that characterized Butter's publications, the Gossips prefer news of a local nature, the sort of news that one can pick up quite easily, and for free, at bakehouses, or in the aisles at Westminster Abbey. As Tattle explains later in the scene, the truthfulness of such reports is relatively immaterial because the primary function of news, as far as she sees it, is to facilitate entertaining, social small talk: "How should we entertain the time else, or find ourselves in fashionable discourse for all companies, if we do not credit all and make more of it for the reporting?" (3.Int.38–41). This frivolous, vapid approach to news is entirely consistent with the Gossips' frivolous, vapid approach to the theater. Jonson's ironic exposition of their absurdly limited perspective establishes a heuristic for interrogating taste across a range of discursive spaces. In addition to parenthetically acknowledging a dialogic relation to the audience, the Gossips' critical commentary enables a comprehensive meditation on the protocols and conventions of the theatrical public that also attempts to engage, and influence, the public created by printed news.

Jonson and the Problem of Interpretation

The Staple of News appeared in print for the first time in a folio edition published by the bookseller Robert Allot in 1631, six years after the premiere performances at the Blackfriars Playhouse. The text is notable for an unusual abundance of prefatory and paratextual material, including a special note to readers and two prologues—one for the court and one for the stage.[24] Like the intermean scenes with the Gossips, these vehicles for authorial interjection show Jonson in an active process of characterizing a space for conversation and promoting standards of taste and behavior.[25] Consider, for example, the detailed portrait of audience activity in "The Prologue for the Stage," which begins by expressing the dramatist's wish to make the audience "wise," by appealing to their "ears," rather than their "eyes"—a pointed reference to his ongoing feud with Inigo Jones over the relative importance of poetry versus spectacle in theatrical production (Jonson believed that one should attend, first and foremost, to the verbal meaning of a dramatic production, not the visual design) (ll. 5–6). Cautioning against the threat of misinterpretation, he offers a lengthy description of the type of behavior that invites distraction:

> You mark [the words of the play] not and sit not still,
> But have a longing to salute or talk
> With such a female, and from her to walk
> With your discourse to what is done, and where.
> How, and by whom, in all the town—but here.
> Alas! What is it to his scene to know
> How many coaches in Hyde Park did show
> Last spring, what fare today at Medley's was,
> If Dunstan or the Phoenix best wine has?
> They are things—but yet, the stage might stand as well
> If it did neither hear these things, nor tell.
>
> (ll. 8–24)

The passage describes a very busy discursive scene: people looking around at each other, waving, and discussing matters such as the coaches at Hyde Park and the wine on offer at various inns around town. Although he contends that "the stage might stand as well" without such chatter, Jonson very clearly has a keen understanding of how the opportunities for public interaction, serious and frivolous alike, contributed to theatrical appeal. The theatergoers he disparages might not be very wise, but they obviously derive some sort of value from their experience—value that has nothing whatsoever to do with the aural import of the drama proper. As the prologue continues, Jonson attributes his audience's appetite for frivolous distraction to the degrading influence of news culture, thereby identifying a connection between news and drama that he will continue to grapple with throughout the play. Insisting on the distinction between true poets, such as himself, and the "poetic elves" who produce news, he argues that the basic ability to produce textual material does not necessarily entail an ability to "think / Conceive, express, and steer the souls of men" (ll. 20–23). Thus, before we get so much as the first line of the first scene, *Staple* articulates the same basic argument that Jonson had been pushing for nearly twenty years: news is a bankrupt form of knowledge, a poor substitute for poetry, and an inadequate platform for addressing matters of social importance.

The choice to print the "Prologue for the Court" directly after the "Prologue for the Stage" presents another important example of theatrical public making in action. In a sense, the dual prologues function in the same way as stamps on a passport: they track where the play has been, thereby concatenating a plurality of physical discursive spaces into a unified print public. On a similar note, by associating the play with the court, Jonson adds an element of what Yachnin refers to as "populuxe"[26] appeal, a sense that readers have become party to an exclusive conversation normally reserved for elites.[27] With these points in mind, it is important to observe that, although the "Prologue to the Court" ostensibly addresses King James, the printed version in fact speaks past the king to a much larger, pseudo-exclusive, audience. Consider, for example, the implications of the following passage, wherein Jonson assures "the King" that the forthcoming play is worthy of his attention by describing the sort of audience it endeavors to reach:

> scholars, that can judge and fair report
> The sense they hear, above the vulgar sort
> Of nutcrackers, that only come for sight.
> Wherein, although our title, sir, be News,
> We yet adventure here to tell you none,
> But show you common follies, and so known,
> That though they are not truths, th'innocent Muse
> Hath made so like, as fant'sy could them state
> Or poetry, without scandal, imitate.
>
> (ll. 6–14)

Once again, Jonson makes a bold declaration of the superiority of verbal meaning over visual spectacle, describing attentive listeners as "scholars, that can judge and fair report," and contrasting them to "nutcrackers, that only come for sight"—an apparent reference to theatergoers in the habit of snacking on nuts during performances (with possible bawdy implications as well).[28] Paradoxically, however, in the simple act of invoking the "nutcrackers," Jonson also acknowledges their place within his discursive community—indeed, in print, the reference functions as a de facto lecture for such persons in theatrical conduct: *attend to the words, ignore the spectacle, and do not create disturbances.* Taking a cue from *News from the New World Discovered in the Moon,* the "Prologue for the Court" also points out that the "news" in *The Staple of News* is not in fact news at all, but poetry that imitates news in order to expose the "common follies" of news culture. Readers hoping to find actual news—in Jonson's theater, or in his playtext—should look elsewhere. Unlike the playtexts for *A Game at Chess,* which seemed to invite association with news by offering a close visual parallel to Scott's *The Second Part of Vox Populi,*[29] Jonson displays an almost paranoid anxiousness to put distance between himself and other forms of print, repeatedly taking care to point out that he is satirizing the news, not relaying it.[30]

The note addressed "To the Readers" suggests that these prefatory disavowals of news culture did not achieve their intended effect. Inserted on page 36 in the space remaining after the second act, the note begins by introducing the forthcoming scene at the Staple, then quickly moves to a stern condemnation of what seems to have been a widespread misinterpretation of the play following the initial performances in 1626:

> In this following Act, the Office is opened and shown to the prodigal and his princess Pecunia, wherein the allegory and purpose of the author hath hitherto been wholly mistaken, and so sinister an interpretation been made, as if the souls of most of the spectators had lived in the eyes and ears of these ridiculous gossips that tattle between the Acts. But he prays you thus to mend it. To consider the news here vented to be none of his news, or any reasonable man's, but news made like the time's news (a weekly cheat to draw money) and could not be finer reprehended than in raising this ridiculous Office of the Staple, wherein the age may see her own folly, or hunger and thirst after published pamphlets of news, set out every Saturday but made all at home, and no syllable of truth in them; than which there cannot be a greater disease in nature, or a fouler scorn put upon the times. And so apprehending it, you shall do the author and your own judgement a courtesy, and perceive the trick of alluring money to the Office and there cozening the people. If you have the truth, rest quiet, and consider that *Ficta voluptatis causa, tint proximo verts.*[31]

As Stuart Sherman has pointed out, the note presents a novel method of authorial intrusion, "a pure print intervention in the midst of a theatrical script, consisting of instructions addressed not to the performers (as in the case of stage directions) nor to the audience (as is often the case in theatrical prologues), but to persons envisioned as ideally absent from the theater and withdrawn from its entire modus operandi."[32] In other words, the note apostrophizes a print public, a community of readers united by common attention to the playtext rather than the theatrical production. More importantly, it also presents one of the most explicit examples in drama of the period where an author steps forward to straightforwardly dictate a "correct" method of interpretation. Although moments of interpretive guidance are characteristic of Jonson (a feature that sets him apart from most early modern dramatists, especially Shakespeare), there is no other work in his corpus that shows him explaining himself quite so adamantly or with the same level of vitriol directed toward his own audience—whom he describes here as "ridiculous" and without reason. On a similar note, the plea for sagacious interpretation also involves an exceptionally powerful attack on the purveyors of early modern news. Significantly, Jonson focuses his ire, not on manuscript newsletters, but on the corantos and news pamphlets published by Butter and Bourne, which by 1631 had become a regular, and very prominent, feature of the print market. Undermining the pretension of these products to reveal an authoritative perspective on world events, he refers to them as "a weekly cheat to draw money," a "disease in nature," and a foul "scorn put upon the times"—containing "no syllable of truth," and "made all at home" (i.e., deriving from no source beyond London). In short, the note represents a radical intensification of the effort Jonson had made in the prologues to position himself at a distance from news culture. Leaving no room whatsoever for "sinister" interpretation, he inserts an unmistakable declaration of purpose directly in front of news parodies that apparently caused misunderstanding in the theater. But why did he feel that such a forceful intervention was necessary?

This question is important to ask because, despite Jonson's candor, the note introduces a number of ambiguities. Specifically, one wonders about the "sinister" interpretations he describes. Although most critics seem to have accepted the claim of gross, widespread misinterpretation at face value,[33] I find it difficult to understand how a majority of the sophisticated theatergoers at the Blackfriars Playhouse could have mistaken the parodic news reports in 3.2 for actual news. The possibility seems even more remote when one considers the presumably successful performance at court of *News from the New World Discovered in the Moon,* which involved similar parodies, and in some cases the exact same jokes. The reception of the material at court must have been somewhat encouraging, or Jonson would not have recycled it for the commercial stage. Of course, there is also the matter of the metatheatrical framing mechanism, which presented the Blackfriars' audience with a caricatured model of how *not* to interpret the play. Jonson is surely exaggerating when he contends that "most spectators" somehow came away from the theater with the same mistaken opinion as the "ridiculous gossips that tattle between the Acts"—but again, why did he feel the exaggeration was necessary? Why did he choose to combine an effort to disassociate himself from news discourse with an effort to disassociate himself from the theatrical audience? One possibility is that he was attempting to deflect blame for a mediocre reception onto a disingenuous public, a theory that seems plausible, but raises the question of why he would want to draw attention to a six-year-old failure in the first place. I suggest that a better answer to the question lies in a tension, theorized by D. F. McKenzie, between Jonson's desire to become a "spokesman for his age" and a competing awareness that his own art had much more in common with the messy realities of news discourse than he preferred to admit.[34] "For all its virtue, [*Staple*] failed in one vital point," McKenzie writes. "It shows no understanding at all of what a painful struggle it is for the ill-educated to learn a new language of conscience and independent political judgment. In deriding their attempts and shutting up his circle against them, Jonson sealed himself off from a world that was becoming uncomfortably intrusive, and in doing so he ceased to be a public poet."[35] Viewed from this angle, Jonson's note to the readers might be read as the product of contrasting impulses: the desire to speak publicly, and the desire to transcend actual public discourse. In order to square these divergent goals, he retreats to an idealized print public, an audience defined in contrast to the public for theater or news—an audience that he can address directly, at any time, from a distance that precludes genuine contact with the vulgar masses.

A News Industry from the Early Modern Near Future

The primary figure of consumption in *The Staple of News* is Pennyboy Jr., a young man who, upon coming of age, has just received (fraudulent) news of his father's passing and looks forward to squandering his inheritance on ostentatious displays of wealth. The play opens to find him at a Fashioner's shop, where a group of tradesmen help to equip him with a suit in the latest style and an accompanying hat, girdle, ruff, cloak, and spurs. Excited by his transformation, he imagines a sense of improved intelligence deriving from his new apparel—an effect that the Fashioner readily confirms:

> Believe it, sir,
> That clothes do much upon the wit, as weather
> Does on the brain; and thence comes your proverb,
> "The tailor makes the man." I speak by experience

Of my own customers. I have had gallants,
Both court and country, would ha' fooled you up,
In a new suit, with the best wits in being,
And kept their speed as long as their clothes lasted
Handsome and neat; but then as they grew out
At the elbows again, or had a stain, or spot,
They have sunk most wretchedly.

(1.2.108–18)

The Fashioner develops a theory of knowledge positing intellectual ability as a product of outward display: the only difference separating "the best wits in being" from persons of lesser intelligence comes down to the quality of one's clothing—appearance equals substance. Ironically undercut by the (presumably) ridiculous image of Pennyboy Jr. in his finery, these comments provide a material analogue for the exploitative approach to language that Jonson problematizes throughout the play. Consider, for example, the prospective "Canting College" discussed in 4.4, an institution that proposes to teach students how to manipulate the specialized vocabularies of various professions so they can fabricate a semblance of actual expertise. Like the Fashioner's theory of clothing and intelligence, the idea for the college follows from a cynical conflation of fashion and substance—a notion that you can make sense out of nonsense by glossing it in a particular style, that all it really takes to become a doctor, for example, is an ability to wield important-sounding medical terminology. Notably, Jonson attacks both the exploiters of language and the credulous consumers whose shallow focus makes exploitation possible. The most prominent example of this dynamic is, of course, the news Staple itself, an institution that enables the dramatist to imagine the future of journalism alongside the logical consequences of unfettered appetite for novelty and fashionability.

Jonson envisioned the Staple in comprehensive detail. Operating out of an elegantly furnished office located in the same house as the Fashioner's shop, the enterprise employs a total of nine persons, including the Master (Cymbal), a Register, an Examiner, two clerks, and four "emissaries" who gather reports from St. Paul's, Westminster, court, and the Exchange (1.5.106–14).[36] When a new report comes in, it is reviewed by the Examiner and filed into an elaborate system of rolls that are organized according to categories such as "news of doubtful credit," "news of the season," "news o' the faction," "Reformed news," "Pontifical news," and so on. (1.5.8–15).[37] Customers place orders with the Register at the front desk, typically specifying a desired category and, in some cases, a price—for example, a customer in 3.2 orders "six pennyworth" of news from Amsterdam (ll. 123–24), and the following customer asks for "news from the Indies" (ll. 53). Following payment, a Staple official reads a report aloud and provides a handwritten copy stamped with an authenticating seal. For an extra fee of two pence per sheet, customers may also purchase a "policy" that offers further proof of origin (1.5.64–66). Notably, these guarantees have nothing to do with the putative truth of the report itself, but function instead as a token of fashionability—they show that the news came from a prestigious source (the Staple), thereby creating a semblance of exclusivity, not unlike the label on a pair of designer jeans.

With the emphasis on exclusivity in view, consider how the Staple employees handle the first customer to appear in the play, an unsophisticated Country Woman with markedly humble, indiscriminate taste in news:

> WOMAN. I would have, sir,
> A groatsworth of any news, I care not what,
> To carry down this Saturday to our vicar.
> REGISTER. Oh, you are a butterwoman. Ask Nathaniel
> The clerk, there.
> NATHANIEL. Sir, I tell her, she must stay
> Till Emissary Exchange or Paul's send in, And then I'll fit her.
> REGISTER. Do, good woman, have patience.
> It is not now as when the captain lived. [*Exit Country Woman.*]
> NATHANIEL. You'll blast the reputation of the office
> Now, I'the bud, if you dispatch these groats
> So soon. Let them attend, in name of policy. (1.4.10–20)

The Register immediately identifies the customer as a "butterwoman" and notes that the days of "the captain" are over, references that associate her with the commercial newsbooks printed by Nathaniel Butter and edited by Captain Thomas Gainsford.[38] Unencumbered by a concern for delicacy, his remarks make it clear that the woman is the sort of customer that he has to keep at a distance—a representative of the vulgar, nonexclusive print public. By forcing her to wait, he endeavors to foster an illusion of exclusivity that distinguishes the news vended at the Staple from news available in print, a purely aesthetic distinction that Jonson, in contrast, wants to deny (which explains why he names the clerk "Nathaniel" after Nathaniel Butter). As Parr has noted, this is the exact same tactic that Lady Pecunia's attendants use to inflate the perceived value of their mistress among her suitors: "'Twill make your grace too cheap," argues Statute, "To give them audience presently" (2.1.59–60).[39] By narrowing—but not entirely blocking—availability, Pecunia's attendants and the Staple employees excite demand, thereby manufacturing value based on nothing more than sheer novelty. For Jonson, this type of value is in fact no value at all—it is the exact opposite of the intellectual worth that he claimed for his own art.

I have paid particular attention to the operational protocol of Cymbal's enterprise in order to foreground two related points that are easy to miss from a distance of four centuries. First, as Muggli has noted, *Staple* is a "prescient portrait of a medium just beginning to coalesce," a futuristic satire that predates the development of industrialized journalism by more than thirty years.[40] This perspective helps to revive a sense of the strangeness and invention inherent in the original production. Although functionaries such as the "Examiner" and the "Emissaries" might seem perfectly ordinary to a twenty-first-century readership familiar with copyeditors and beat reporters, such jobs were a fanciful prophecy in 1626, a fiction that Jonson came up with by considering the form that a full-blown industry based on the commodification of information might assume. In the process of developing his window onto the future of news, he cobbled together various details from actual institutions in Jacobean society, including the process of examination and registration employed by the Stationer's Company, and the process of newsgathering and dissemination employed by the Office of Posts and Couriers.[41] In short, the enterprise is a pastiche, and has no single parallel in Jacobean culture—an observation that brings me to my second, more important, point: Jonson's satire focuses primarily on *ideas,* rather than specific persons or media. Although criticism has tended to frame the play as a direct attack on the printed news products published by Butter and Bourne, *Staple* is in fact a much more comprehensive indictment of the attitudes and assumptions underlying news culture in general. By interpreting the play in terms of ideas rather than possible topical referents, one can begin to see the underlying connection between elements that might otherwise suggest contradiction or confusion. For example, as noted in the foregoing paragraphs, the Staple employees offer news in two forms—oral and manuscript, *not* print—and make a point of keeping less sophisticated members of the print public at a distance. In this respect, the enterprise bears a strong resemblance to the private manuscript news services provided by professional letter writers such as John Chamberlain or the Factor in *News from the New World Discovered in the Moon*—but that is only half the story. On the other hand, there is also an abundance of details linking the Staple to commercially printed news, including more than twenty references to the name "Butter," and a number of specific references to the rhetoric of corantos and newssheets (more on this point in the following section). To square these ostensible contradictions, one must recognize that, above and beyond any single contemporary target in particular, Jonson wants to get at a news-oriented way of thinking about the world. From his point of view, manuscript newsletters, newsy gossip, and printed news documents were all equally conducive to the growing influence of false knowledge, a phenomenon that he blames for the increasingly degraded state of social discourse. In effect, his Staple functions in much the same way as Shakespeare's Autolycus in *The Winter's Tale:* it is a reification of the *concept* of news—an amalgamation of diverse elements and ideas expressed as a coherent dramatic figuration.

News and Mock News

In act 3, Pennyboy Jr. takes Lady Pecunia to the Staple office and attempts to impress her by spending extravagantly on news of "any kind. / So it be news, the newest that thou hast" (3.2.18–19). His willingness to purchase anything, no matter how ridiculous, initiates a rapid-fire succession of reports delivered by Nathaniel, Fitton (the emissary to court), and Thomas (Pennyboy Jr.'s former barber, now working as a Staple clerk). Approximately halfway through the scene, a group of news-hungry customers enter in a flurry of excitement, soliciting another wave of reports. There are seventeen stories in total:

1. On "the thirtieth of February," the king of Spain was appointed both pope and emperor (a story that mocks the tendency of polemical pamphleteers to refer to Spain and Rome as a unified Catholic monolith) (ll. 21–22).[42] The former emperor has resigned and now serves as a foot soldier under Johann Tzerclas, Count of Tilly, commander of the forces of the Catholic League (ll. 23–25).
2. On a similar note, the infamous Spanish military leader Don Ambrogio Spinola Doria has become general of the Jesuits and has devised a variety of new weapons, including an engine "to wind himself up to the moon" and explosive eggs capable of destroying an entire city (ll. 26–52).[43]

3. Galileo has developed a magnifying glass that can focalize moonlight and burn enemy ships from a distance (ll. 53–56).
4. Cornelius Drebbel (a Dutch inventor) has devised an "invisible eel" that can swim under water and attack Spanish ships from below (ll. 59–86).
5. The "eel" may prove ineffective, however, because Spinola has organized an army that floats above water on cork carriages (ll. 86–93).
6. The Rosicrucians have perfected "the art of drawing farts out of dead bodies" (ll. 87–104).
7. An alewife in Saint Katherine's has discovered "perpetual motion" at her alehouse: the customers never stop drinking (ll. 105–9).
8. The Anabaptists in Amsterdam are expecting the arrival of a prophet with the ability to predict the future (ll. 123–39).[44]
9. The sultan of the Ottoman Empire, Murad IV Ghazi, has cut ties with the pope, converted to Christianity, and made plans to visit the Anabaptist church in Amsterdam (ll. 140–52).[45]
10. A group of cooks will establish a new colony on the coast of America in order to make "good-eating Christians" out of the "cannibals" (ll. 153–79).
11. The king's barber has initiated a royal proclamation prohibiting long hairstyles for men (ll. 186–198).
12. The archbishop of Spalato has left a legacy to the players who impersonated him in *A Game at Chess* (Spalato was the model for the Fat Bishop) (ll. 200–205).
13. The Spanish ambassador, Gondomar (another figure impersonated in *Game*), has given himself a second anal fistula after using "the poor English play that was writ of him" to wipe his "posteriors" (ll. 206–14).[46]
14. Gabriel Bethlen, the Prince of Transylvania, has devised a drum that can be heard throughout "all Christendom"—it is so loud, in fact, that it threatens to deafen his soldiers, thereby obliging the prince to employ a "design" for transporting his army in the sky (ll. 285–92).
15. Maximilian, the elector of Bavaria, has become "the Church's miller," and "grinds the Catholic grist / with every wind" (a reference to the military support offered by Maximilian to Catholic forces in the Palatinate, despite a treaty with the Protestant Union) (ll. 294–97).
16. The guildsmen expected to make speeches at pageants for the coronation of Charles I have been struck mute, and stand frozen

like wooden blocks (a reference to the unusually sparse levels of pageantry that accompanied the coronation of Charles I due to a breakout of plague) (ll. 298–306).

17. Construction is underway on a new park that will separate cuckolds with impressive horns from cuckolds with horns of lesser quality (ll. 307–12).

In the space of less than three hundred lines, Jonson mentions sixteen specific newsmakers and numerous other groups, events, obsessions, and quirks associated with contemporary news discourse, thereby producing one of the most dense concentrations of topical references in all of early modern drama. With this complexity in view, it is important to note that, while the brief summary offered in the foregoing paragraph helps to clarify the scene, it also threatens to elide an important aspect of the intended effect: obscurity is an element of Jonson's design, an integral part of how he establishes meaning and tone. Ultimately, the satirical import hinges on the force of a cumulative impression—Jonson wants to create a generalized representation of the way news sounds, the fuss it makes over frivolities, and the illogical manner in which it skips from item to item without ever pausing for verification or reflection. In pursuit of this objective, he takes significant care to re-create the language and decorum of contemporary news discourse in significant detail. To get a sense of the news-oriented resonance of his imitation, consider the appendix, which lists the names that appear most frequently in the extant title pages of the newsbooks published by Nathaniel Butter and his colleagues between 1623 and 1626.[47] As I have noted, *Staple* 3.2 makes reference to no less than five of the top ten persons on the list—an indication that Jonson was picking names that carried maximal associative impact, purposefully evoking the linguistic particularities of discourse centered on news. The same is also true for the places mentioned in the mock reports and the inventions, intrigues, and phenomena they describe. In short, the scene presents what one might think of as an affective adaptation—the bewildering experience of early modern news discourse reimagined as a coherent dramatic expression.

As is always the case with Jonson, satire directed at the rhetoric of news also exposes the credulity and vapidity of news consumers: "Is't true?" asks Pennyboy Jr. in response to the report of Spinola's floating army (3.2.92). "As true as the rest," replies Fitton—and the discussion of truthfulness ends there, making way for an equally fatuous report about mystic methods for extracting intestinal gas from cadavers (3.2.92). Like Mopsa and Dorcas in *The Winter's Tale* 4.3, Pennyboy Jr.'s requirements for belief require no assurances beyond a slight, pro forma gesture toward veracity. He merely wants to *feel* like an informed sophisticate, and to project a semblance of knowledgeability to others—the actual quality of the knowledge he purportedly possesses is only important insofar as it impinges on a tenuous surface appearance. Thus, as far as he is concerned, actual truth and the word "truth" amount to the exact same thing: Fitton says the news is true, and so it is, and there is no reason to consider the matter in any more depth than that. The ironic implication of the emissary's guarantee—that the report is "as true as the rest," that is, not true at all—does not register because it operates beyond the parameters of an uncritical, purely literal mind-set. As in *Volpone* and *News from the New World Discovered in the Moon,* Jonson suggests that, if the value of language resides entirely in the superficial ability of words to excite fleeting fascination, then irony, and nuanced meaning in general, counts for nothing.

The familiar emphasis in *Staple* 3.2 on an appetitive, unthinking consumer base brings me to some final thoughts on Jonson's complex attitude toward publicity in general. One of the most significant passages in this regard occurs when the Register gives Pennyboy Jr. a brief description of the scene he is about to behold as the customers who have been kept waiting outside begin to enter:

> 'Tis the House of Fame, sir,
> Where both the curious and the negligent,
> The scrupulous and careless, wild and staid,
> The idle and laborious, all do meet
> To taste the cornucopiae of her rumours,
> Which she, the mother of sport, pleaseth to scatter
> Among the vulgar. Baits, sir, for the people!
> And they will bite like fishes.
>
> (3.2.115–22)

By describing the Staple as "the House of Fame," the Register makes a direct connection between news and the classical notion of *fama,* or the indiscriminate circulation of all public discourse—including truth, slander, rumor, gossip, reputation, and infamy.[48] In Jonson's iteration, the idea of disorganized, intermingling discourses also involves the physical convergence of different sorts of people, a heterogeneous congregation caught up in the process of circulating the news. Notably, rather than referring to typical markers, such as profession or social station, the Register characterizes the individual members of this collective in terms of their attitude toward the consumption of information: "the curious and the negligent, / The scrupulous and careless, [the] wild and staid, / The idle and laborious." One might find it tempting to discover an argument for the democratizing potential of public discourse in the notion of a discursive space that supplants social categories with categories of intellectual inclination, but Jonson was not Habermas—he did not see anything positive in the unfettered availability of information, and democracy probably would have struck him as a profoundly ill-conceived idea. Indeed, the tone of the passage suggests that there is something distinctly unsavory about the radical availability of the Staple, a forum where "vulgar" adherents "bite like fishes" at any bait that Rumor "pleaseth to scatter." If the news-hungry mob that appears in the middle of 3.2 is an image of a nascent public sphere, as a number of commentators have suggested,[49] then it is a nightmare vision, a grave prediction of the catastrophic consequences that an increase in opportunities for public participation would inevitably yield. As I have argued throughout the chapter, this view of publicity puts pressure on Jonson's claim for the superiority and separateness of his own art, a pressure that he is very obviously aware of. One cannot help but notice, after all, that the mob at the Staple bears an unmistakable resemblance to the Gossips who burst on stage at the beginning of the play and the "vulgar nutcrackers" derided in the prologue. Despite his efforts to establish himself at a distance from these uncouth, overeager public participants, Jonson was inextricably invested in the social shift that made their participation possible.

"Invested" is a particularly appropriate word to use in this context because, as Yachnin has pointed out, Jonson was not only a critic of news culture, but was also a retailer of news whose populuxe business model hinged on the perceived ability of theatrical experience to emulate the discourse of courtly elites.[50] On a related note, I would add that Butter and Gainsford's business model worked along very similar lines: the corantos and newsbooks of the 1620s derived from private, manuscript newsletters and marketed themselves as such, thereby making their connection to the discourse of elites a key point of sale—as Gossip Tattle straightforwardly asserts, early moderns went to the theater to hear news and bought printed news products for purposes of social recreation (Induction 25–27; 3.Int.38–41). Attention to the populuxe nature of both forms opens up another way of understanding the concentration of news references in *Staple* 3.2: regardless of their satirical intention, Jonson's mock news stories traded on the same body of discourse as any other commercial news product, channeled the appeal of the same celebrities, and capitalized on the same pool of interests. *Staple* sold access to a conversation about news that held value as a form of entertainment and as a vehicle of social prestige. Considered from this angle, 3.2 seems a little bit less like a scathing condemnation of news culture, and a little bit more like an especially novel and prominent example of a dramatist providing his audience with the news talk they had paid to hear.

I want to end my analysis of *Staple* by emphasizing Jonson's dual role as *both* populuxe newsmonger and serious news critic, not because I think there is anything exploitative or insincere about his analysis, but, on the contrary, because I think the ability of drama to reflexively comment on an industry that it was also a part of is directly pertinent to my theory of how the theater contributed to an expansion of the idea of news. Writing about the same type of duality in Middleton's *The Witch,* Yachnin notes that the play's "literary capacity to develop a self-consciousness" relatively detached from its institutional "embeddedness in the entertainment market" exemplifies the capacity of theatrical art to "provide both an experience of courtliness and a critical representation of that experience," a feature that "distinguishes it from other forms of recreation such as visiting prostitutes or imbibing wine."[51] *Staple,* with its multiple prologues, metatheatrical chorus, and various other reflexive mechanisms—all functioning at a critical distance from a strong orientation toward the market for news—offers a notable example of this capacity for semiautonomous self-awareness in operation. Jonson provided his readers and spectators with a commercial entertainment product that held value as a form of news and as a form of vicarious engagement with elite culture. By trading on these attractions, he contributed to the cultivation of the ideas and practices undergirding their commercial viability, and also helped to foster a market wherein they could count as salable goods—it is not surprising, therefore, to find *Staple* capitalizing on the same celebrities and issues that drove the publishing practices of printers such as Butter and Bourne. Moreover, as a literary creation, the play also had unique representative capabilities that enabled it to step outside the market framework, to a certain extent, and to reflect critically on the courtliness and news-centeredness that it held up for sale. It was fundamentally *of* the market, but also *about* the market—a prominent, salable product, but also a meaningful intellectual exercise that facilitated a thoughtful, playful expansion of the idea of news.

Epilogue: News Is What They Say It Is

Andrew Pettegree sums up his formidable history of news production in early modern Europe by observing that the "news media of [the] era presented every bit as much a multi-media phenomenon as our own. It is that which gives this period its particular fascination."[1] Building on this observation, I would add that, in the seventeenth century as in the twenty-first, the proliferation and cultivation of news in fact *depended,* not only on a multiplicity of media platforms, but also on a multiplicity of vehicles for sharing, feeling, and thinking through topical discourse, vehicles that ranged from relatively straightforward reportage to more artistic forms such as balladry and dramatic performance. As the foregoing chapters have repeatedly asserted, news is not a one-way broadcast that travels from senders to receivers, but a massive public conversation that derives relevancy and force from a network sustained by cultural producers—the people who write, sing, dance, joke, rhyme, paint, and otherwise make the discourse that propels the conversation forward. I would also add that an appreciation of the basic functional affinity between news in early modernity and news today is not only fascinating, but in fact essential to an understanding of how conventional news sources operate in relation to other forms in the overall media ecology. For example, there is a strong parallel between Ben Jonson's satirical dramas and the topical monologues delivered on late-night comedy programs, which typically do double duty as entertainment and media critique. Carrying the argument slightly further, one can also begin to see how forms such as Jacobean city comedies, revenge tragedies, and historical drama bear a similar historical kinship to sitcoms, television dramas, and other sources of popular entertainment in our own age. News is what these forms say it is, not only because they make a significant contribution to the overall circulation of news discourse, but also because they exert a fundamental influence on what the news means, how it feels, and why it matters.

Of course, one might argue that a late-night comedy show or television drama is not in fact "making" news at all because it is merely riffing on information originally reported in newspapers or other conventional sources. In response, I would suggest that such a view is only persuasive insofar as one accepts the misleading image of news production that the factuality-centered posture of professional journalism implicitly asserts—the illusion, in other words, that news is a transparent window on the world, untainted by any sort of mitigation. As I argued in chapter 1, the process of news making is actually much more creative and proactive: it links select slices of perceived reality together and arranges them into a narrative framework. The crucial point to grasp here is that news making is not a process of simply unearthing raw information, or pulling a curtain back to reveal the true world, but a process of cultivating and contributing to an ongoing public conversation centered on current events. A topical monologue by a late-night talk show host exerts influence over the news public by offering a perspective that is approachable and fun, but is also conducive to critical reflection because it approaches conventional news talk from an elucidating distance. The theater of Shakespeare, Middleton, and Jonson served a similar function in the emergent news culture of seventeenth-century London.

Attention to the concurrent evolution of news and drama provides a historical model for how news culture continues to work today, and also provides a significant new perspective on the discursive situation of early modern England. As I have shown, the two forms emerged around the same time, offered complementary opportunities for participation in public discussion, cultivated a common audience, traded on a similar notion of value, and worked in conjunction with one another to expand and refine ideas at the foundation of the social imaginary—most notably, a new and significantly more sophisticated idea of news itself. The development of the new idea of news was an extraordinarily important literary and cultural innovation: rather than positing current events in terms of an isolated, static, historical past—as was the case with older forms of news discourse—it brought subjects into dialogue with a massive, ongoing conversation, a rush of information that is always changing and always happening "right now" across a vast, interconnected world. My analysis has shown three of the most important and influential dramatists of the period interacting with the idea in a variety of respects.

In closing, I want to offer a few general thoughts on the benefits that I hope my research has opened up for future scholarship. First and foremost, the work has helped me see the importance of reading early modern news and drama alongside each other, not simply for purposes of source studies, but in order to gain a sharper understanding of the expanding contemporary conversation that both forms cultivated and depended on for viability. On a related note, it has also demonstrated the formative role that mechanisms other than conventional news documents played in the development of news culture, thus pointing the way toward a new manner of thinking about the history of news. This point is particularly relevant in regard to drama, as I have argued, but also applies to other forms of public discourse such as sermons and ballads—frameworks that enabled people to look at the news from different angles and think about it in new ways.

Finally, I hope my work has provided a striking and original example of how early modern artistic practices helped to create the public culture and also helped to bring about far-reaching social change. The drama produced by professional playing companies in the first quarter of the seventeenth century added to the conceptual infrastructure for an idea of news that would have a profound impact on public discourse in the following centuries, and continues to shape how we think about our position in society and our relation to current events in the present era. Notably, this accomplishment came about, not because the players envisioned themselves as agents of social change (some did, others did not), and not because they commanded direct political influence (they did not), but because theatrical experience had a unique ability to bring people together into new sorts of discursive communities, and to inspire imaginative conversations that opened up new ways of thinking about the world. Ultimately, the idea of news is an idea about publicity, an idea that there are other people "out there," engaged in an ongoing conversation that is open to everyone and constantly changing as it moves forward in time. As purveyors of news, the early modern dramatists were actively involved in the promotion of this way of looking at the world—or what I have called "news thinking"—as a viable, valuable form of knowledge, and also as a form of entertainment. Moreover, as literary artists, they significantly broadened and enriched the discursive field wherein news thinking played out, providing elements such as critical self-awareness, playful openness, and emotional depth. In early modern London, news was what Shakespeare, Middleton, and Jonson said it was—not only because they were central to the emergent news culture, but also because their art helped to define the very concept of news itself.

Appendix: Names Frequently Used in Butter Newsbooks, 1623–1626

The following is a list of the twenty persons most frequently referred to in the seventy-three extant title pages of newsbooks published by Nathaniel Butter and his colleagues from 1623 to 1626. It derives from Folke Dahl's *Bibliography of English Corantos and Periodical Newsbooks, 1620–1642*. The names of persons referred to in *The Staple of News* 3.2 are in bold.

1. **Gabriel Bethlen,** king of Hungary, Prince of Transylvania, Duke of Opole—leader of an anti-Habsburg insurrection in the Habsburg Royal Hungary; Protestant hero (aka "Bethlem Gabor," "Gabor"). 41 references.
2. **Ferdinand II,** Holy Roman emperor, king of Bohemia, and king of Hungary (aka "the Emperor," "Ferdinand"). 40 references.
3. Ernst von Mansfeld, German military commander (aka "Mansfield"). 40 references.
4. **Johann Tzerclas, Count of Tilly**, commander of the forces of the Catholic League (aka "Tilly"). 32 references.
5. Christian the Younger, Duke of Brunswick-Lüneburg and bishop of Halberstadt, German military commander (aka "Brunswick"). 27 references.
6. Christian IV, king of Denmark. 19 references.
7. **Don Ambrogio Spinola Doria,** first Marquis of the Balbases, leader of the Spanish army in the Netherlands (aka "Spinola," "Don Spinola"). 18 references.

8. Maurice of Nassau, Prince of Orange. 18 references.
9. **Murad IV Ghazi,** sultan of the Ottoman Empire (aka "the Great Turk," "the Grand Signor"). 9 references.
10. Charles Emmanuel I, Duke of Savoy. 8 references.
11. Count von Anholt, a lieutenant under Johann Tzerclas, Count of Tilly. 8 references.
12. Louis XIII, king of France. 8 references.
13. Gonzalo Fernández de Córdoba, Spanish military leader. 8 references.
14. **Philip IV,** king of Spain (aka "the King of Spain," "Philip"). 7 references.
15. The Marquis Jagersdorf, ally of Gabriel Bethlen. 6 references.
16. **Pope Urban VIII** (aka "the Pope," "Pope Barbarino," "Maffeo Barberini"). 6 references.
17. Pope Gregory XV, predecessor to Pope Urban VIII (aka "the Pope"). 6 references.
18. Mustafa I Deli, sultan of the Ottoman Empire, predecessor to Murad IV Ghazi (aka "the Great Turk," "the Grand Signor"). 5 references.
19. **Maximilian, Duke of Bavaria**, founder of the Catholic League and champion of Ferdinand II (aka "Maximilian," "the Duke of Bavier"). 4 references.
20. François Annibal d'Estrées, Marquis de Coeuvres, French military commander. 4 references.

Notes

Acknowledgments

1. The episode is available for download here: http://www.cbc.ca/ideas/episodes/2014/06/05/ideas-from-the-trenches-the-theatre-of-news/.

Chapter 1

1. Gurr, *Playgoing in Shakespeare's London* (Cambridge: Cambridge University Press, 1987), 4.

2. Note, however, that private networks for circulating manuscript newsletters among persons of quality were already long established by this time, and continued to exist alongside commercial news well into the seventeenth century. These letters typically focused on events at court or foreign wars. Despite their ostensible exclusivity, the narratives they carried regularly trickled down into more widely accessible news forms, sometimes verbatim. For example, see my analysis of *Heuy newes* later in this chapter. On manuscript culture and the origins of news culture see Sabrina A. Baron, "The Guises of Dissemination in Early Seventeenth-Century England," in *The Politics of Information in Early Modern Europe*, ed. Brendan Dooley and Sabrina A. Baron (London: Routledge, 2001), 41–57; Alastair Bellany, *The Politics of Court Scandal in Early Modern England: News Culture and the Overbury Affair, 1603–1660* (Cambridge: Cambridge University Press, 2002); Harold Love, *Scribal Publication in Seventeenth-Century England* (Oxford: Clarendon, 1993); Peter Lake and Steven C. A. Pincus, eds., *The Politics of the Public Sphere in Early Modern England* (Manchester: Manchester University Press, 2007); Peter Lake and Michael C. Questier, *The Antichrist's Lewd Hat: Protestants, Papists and Players in Post-Reformation England* (New Haven: Yale University Press, 2002); and F. J. Levy, "How Information Spread among the Gentry, 1550–1640," *Journal of British Studies* 21, no. 2 (1982): 11–34.

3. Jackie Harrison, *News* (London: Routledge, 2006), 285.

4. H. L. Rogers, "An English Tailor and Father Garnet's Straw," *Review of English Studies* 16, no. 61 (1965): 44–45.

5. See Alden T. Vaughan, "William Strachey's 'True Reportory' and Shakespeare: A Closer Look at the Evidence," *Shakespeare Quarterly* 59, no. 3 (2008): 245–73.

6. A notable example along similar lines is *The Plantation of Virginia* (1623), an anonymous, lost play that may have dramatized the massacre of Virginian colonists by aboriginals in 1622 (see Claire Jowitt, *Voyage Drama and Gender Politics, 1589–1642: Real and Imagined Worlds* [Manchester: Manchester University Press, 2003], 201–2). Around the same time, Dekker, Webster, Rowley, and Ford collaborated on another lost play entitled *Late Murder in White Chapel, or Keep the Widow Waking* (1624), which dramatized two contemporary London crime scandals: the coerced marriage of Anne Elsdon (an elderly widow) to Tobias Audley, and the murder of Joan Tindall by her young son, John Tindall (see Charles J. Sisson, *Lost Plays of Shakespeare's Age* [Cambridge: Cambridge University Press, 1936], 80–110).

7. For an elaboration of the generally dismissive attitude of authority toward drama, see Paul Yachnin, "The Powerless Theatre," *English Literary Renaissance* 21, no. 1 (1991): 49–74.

8. On "functional ambiguity" see Annabel M. Patterson, *Censorship and Interpretation: The Conditions of Writing and Reading in Early Modern England* (Madison: University of Wisconsin Press, 1984), 3–23.

9. Martin Wiggins, *Shakespeare and the Drama of His Time* (Oxford: Oxford University Press, 2000), 106.

10. Robert Gell to Sir Martin Stuteville, 9 August 1628; anonymous newsletter of 8 August 1628, Isham of Lamport Manuscript Collection, Northamptonshire Record Office (NRO), MS IL 2671, fol. 1v; anonymous newsletter of 8 August 1628, Isham of Lamport MSS, NRO MS IL 2671, fol. 2r.

11. Thomas Cogswell and Peter Lake, "Buckingham Does the Globe: *Henry VIII* and the Politics of Popularity in the 1620s," *Shakespeare Quarterly* 60, no. 3 (2009): 253–78.

12. Gurr, *Playgoing in Shakespeare's London*, 118.

13. Of course, there are other important platforms that made a significant contribution to the overall news culture, most notably the various spaces connected to the Church of England. My emphasis is on how aspects such as voluntary participation, a sense of play, and imaginative, emotional engagement made theatrical space a genuinely unique and innovative space for news thinking and public involvement.

14. David Cressy, "Literacy in Seventeenth-Century England," *Journal of Interdisciplinary History* 8 (1977): 144–64: Cressy estimates that that the illiteracy rate for the early seventeenth century was somewhere around 70 percent (p. 144).

15. Extensive records detailing the movements of London's touring companies survive to this day. For more information, see *REED: Records of Early English Drama*, http://link.library.utoronto.ca/reed/index.cfm.

16. Zachary Lesser, *Renaissance Drama and the Politics of Publication: Readings in the English Book Trade* (Cambridge: Cambridge University Press, 2004), 115–56.

17. Ibid., 208.

18. John Hartley, *Understanding News* (London: Methuen, 1982), 11.

19. Daniel Woolf, "News, History, and the Construction of the Present in Early Modern England," in Dooley and Baron, *Politics of Information*, 98.

20. Ibid.

21. Note, however, that Habermas is also very skeptical about most forms of media and particularly concerned about the distortive, antidemocratic influence of adver-

tising and public relations (a theme he develops in the second part of *The Structural Transformation of the Public Sphere*).

22. Jürgen Habermas, *The Structural Transformation of the Public Sphere: An Inquiry into a Category of Bourgeois Society*, tr. Thomas Burger (Cambridge, MA: MIT Press, 1989), 24.

23. David Cayley, "The Origins of the Modern Public Episode 13: Publics and Counterpublics," *Ideas*, CBC, 23 June 2010, *iTunes Podcasts*, accessed 1 September 2010.

24. Craig J. Calhoun, *Habermas and the Public Sphere* (Cambridge, MA: MIT Press, 1992), 37–38.

25. Ibid.

26. Bronwen Wilson and Paul Yachnin, *Making Publics in Early Modern Europe: People, Things, Forms of Knowledge* (New York: Routledge, 2010), 1.

27. Ibid.

28. *Heuy Newes of an Horryble Earth Quake whiche was in the Cytie of Scharbaria in this Present Yeare of. XLII. The XIII. Day of June. Also how that a Cytie in Turky is Sonke* (London, 1622), 8.

29. Ibid., 3.

30. Ibid.

31. Anthony Parr, ed., *The Staple of News* (Manchester: Manchester University Press, 1999), 24.

32. *Heuy Newes*, 4.

33. Folke Dahl, *A Bibliography of English Corantos and Periodical Newsbooks, 1620–1642* (London: Bibliographical Society, 1952), 55.

34. Michael Warner, *Publics and Counterpublics* (New York: Zone Books, 2002), 62.

35. *The Strangling and Death of the Great Turke, and his two Sonnes With the Strange Preservation and Deliverance of his Vncle Mustapha from Perishing in Prison, with Hunger and Thirst, the Young Emperour Now Three Dayes before Having so Commanded* (London, 1622), A3v.

36. Ibid.

37. Ibid., B4v; qtd. in Dahl, *Bibliography of English Corantos*, 70.

38. Warner, *Publics and Counterpublics*, 71.

39. Ibid., 71.

40. *The Affaires of Italy, with the Crowning and Inauguration of the New Pope Barbarino a Florentine in Rome, and Other Accidents* (London, 1623), A3v; qtd. in Marcus Nevitt, "Ben Jonson and the Serial Publication of News," *Media History* 11 (2005): 60.

41. Dahl, *Bibliography of English Corantos*, 149.

42. *Late Newes or True Relations*, 30 (London, 1624), A3.

43. Nevitt, "Ben Jonson," 58.

Chapter 2

1. All references to Shakespeare's works are taken from *The Complete Works of Shakespeare*, ed. David Bevington, 6th ed. (New York: Pearson Longman, 2006).

2. See http://www.opensourceshakespeare.org/concordance/.

3. Ian Atherton, "The Itch Grown a Disease: Manuscript Transmission of News in the Seventeenth Century," in *News, Newspapers, and Society in Early Modern Britain*, ed. Joad Raymond (Portland: Frank Cass, 1999), 39–43.

4. These lists of examples are not comprehensive.

5. The figure of Rumor derives from the classical idea of *fama*, a word that combines all forms of public discourse, good and bad, true and untrue, alike. Fama is personified in a number of classical sources, most notably in Virgil's *Aeneid* 4.173–78 and in book 12 of Ovid's *Metamorphoses*. Shakespeare was also undoubtedly familiar with Chaucer's poem *The House of Fame*, which makes use of the same idea.

6. The image of multiple tongues as a metonymy for rumor may have had an added salience at the end of the sixteenth century. In 1596, the year before *2 Henry IV* likely appeared at the Globe, Edmund Spenser published *The Second Part of the Faerie Queen*, which memorably features a hundred-tongued dog named "The Blatant Beast," an allegory for slander and gossip that bears striking similarities to Shakespeare's Rumor (see book VI, canto xii).

7. Note that Jonson makes a similar connection between news culture and the classical idea of *fama* in *The Staple of News* 3.2.115–22.

8. On the messengers in *Antony and Cleopatra* see also C. C. Barfoot, "News of the Roman Empire: Hearsay, Soothsay, Myth and History in *Antony and Cleopatra*," in *Reclamations of Shakespeare*, ed. A. J. Hoenselaars (Amsterdam: Rodopi, 1994), 103–28.

9. Janet Adelman, *The Common Liar: An Essay on "Antony and Cleopatra"* (New Haven: Yale University Press, 1973), 35, 34.

10. Ibid., 39.

11. John Pitcher, "Some Call Him Autolycus," in *In Arden: Editing Shakespeare. Essays in Honour of Richard Proudfoot*, ed. Ann Thompson and Gordon McMullan (London: Arden Shakespeare, 2003), 578–79. Pitcher argues that Autoclyus's claim to have served the Prince is an obvious, "bare-faced lie" that "must have been greeted by laughter and catcalls from the audience in the Globe." Elsewhere, he notes that the attempt to "dupe the audience" demonstrates a unique depth of dishonesty: unlike other soliloquizing vice figures, such as Iago, he seems to have an absolute inability to tell the truth, even when he is expressing his innermost thoughts in a soliloquy (John Pitcher, ed., *The Winter's Tale* [London: Arden Shakespeare, 2010], 75).

12. Forman wrote the only extant eyewitness report of the original production of the *Winter's Tale* at the Globe. After sketching the primary plot, he dedicates approximately a third of his short account to a description of Autolycus: "Remember also the Rog that cam in all tottered like coll pixci/. and how he feyned hime sick & to haue bin Robbed of all that he had and howe he cosoned the por man of all his money. and after cam to the shep sher with a pedlers pack & ther cosoned them Again of all their money And howe he changed apparell w[t] the king of bomia his sonn and then howe he turned Coutiar &c / beware of trustinge feined beggars or fawninge fellouss" (from Forman's manuscript *The Bocke of Plaies and Notes thereof per Formans for Common Pollicie*, reprinted by John H. P. Pafford in his Arden edition of *The Winter's Tale*: John H. P. Pafford, ed., *The Winter's Tale* (London: Methuen, 1963), xxi–xxii.

13. On Autolycus and masterless men, see Lake and Questier, *The Antichrist's Lewd Hat*, 119, 468; and Barbara A. Mowat, "Rogues, Shepherds, and the Counterfeit Distressed: Texts and Infracontexts of *The Winter's Tale* 4.3," *Shakespeare Studies* 22 (1994): 70.

14. From *Metamorphoses* II.303–17. Quoted by Orgel in his introduction to *The Winter's Tale*: Stephen Orgel, ed., *The Winter's Tale* (New York: Oxford University Press, 1998), 50.

15. Andrew Fleck, "Vulgar Fingers of the Multitude: Shakespeare, Jonson, and the Transformation of News from the Low Countries," *Shakespeare Yearbook* 15 (2005): 91–92, 96–97.

16. See Joad Raymond, *Pamphlets and Pamphleteering in Early Modern Britain* (Cambridge: Cambridge University Press, 2003), 128; Edward Arber, ed., *A Transcript of the Registers of the Company of Stationers of London: 1554–1640 A.D.*, 5 vols. (London: Privately Printed, 1875–94), 3.241, 303; and M. A. Shaaber, *Some Forerunners of the Newspaper in England, 1476–1622* (Philadelphia: University of Pennsylvania Press, 1929), 310–11.

17. For information on the dating of Donne's epigrams, see Gary A. Stringer, ed., *The Variorum Edition of the Poetry of John Donne* (Bloomington: Indiana University Press, 1995), 8.281.

18. Stringer, ed., *Poetry of John Donne*, 8.5. This epigram is also cited by Raymond, *Pamphlets and Pamphleteering*, 128–29, and by Fleck, "Vulgar Fingers of the Multitude," 91.

19. "Aesop was sold as a slave along with two other men. The prospective purchaser asked each what he knew how to do. The others replied 'everything,' but Aesop replied 'nothing,' explaining that the others had already claimed all knowledge for themselves." John Donne, *The Satires, Epigrams and Verse Letters*, ed. Wesley Milgate (Oxford: Clarendon Press, 1967), 201.

20. A. J. Smith, ed., *The Complete English Poems of John Donne* (Harmondsworth: Penguin, 1971), 467.

21. Natascha Würzbach, *The Rise of the English Street Ballad, 1550–1650* (Cambridge: Cambridge University Press, 2010), 4.

22. Fleck, "Vulgar Fingers of the Multitude," 97.

23. Würzbach, *Rise of the English Street Ballad*, 1.

24. Shaaber, *Some Forerunners*, 193–94.

25. This point marks a significant departure from Shaaber, *Some Forerunners*, which seems to exclude the possibility of meaningful public life.

26. Orgel notes that a tune with this title was circulating around 1610. The lyrics have not survived. From the servant's description it seems to have been structured as a dialogue between a man and a woman, with "the man's incipient ribaldry repeatedly cut short" by the woman's refrain, "Whoop, me no harm, good man!" The suggestion of bawdiness—a common feature of broadside ballads—is also indicated by "dildos" and "fadings," which function as nonsense words in this context, but also carry sexual overtones (a "fading" was a type of jig); see notes, Orgel, ed., *The Winter's Tale*, 179–80).

27. Hyder E. Rollins, "The Black-Letter Broadside Ballad," *PMLA* 34, no. 2 (1919): 308–9. On a similar note, Robert Greene describes a balladeer working in cooperation with a pickpocket at the doors of a commercial playhouse: Robert Greene, *The Third and Last part of Conny-Catching. With the new Deuised Knauish Arte of Foole-Taking. The like Coosnages and Villanies Neuer Before Discouered* (London, 1592).

28. Stephen Gosson, *The Schoole of Abuse, Conteining a Pleasunt Inuective Against Poets Pipers, Plaiers, Jesters and such like Catterpillers of a Commonwealth (1579)*, ed. Edward Arber (London: English Reprints, 1868), 70. This quotation is from Natascha Würzbach's very helpful collection of contemporary references to ballads and balladeers, *Rise of the English Street Ballad*, 262.

29. Angela McShane-Jones, "*The Gazet in Metre; Or The Rhiming Newsmonger*: The English Broadside Ballad as Intelligencer: A New Narrative," in *News and Politics in Early Modern Europe (1500–1800)*, ed. Joop W. Koopmans (Leuven: Peeters, 2005), 131–51.

30. Würzbach, *Rise of the English Street Ballad*, 14.

31. The full title of Gosson's book, in all its rhetorical glory, is *The Schoole of Abuse Contayning a Pleasaunt Inuectiue against Poets, Pipers, Players, Iesters, and such like Caterpillers of a Common Wealth; Setting Vp the Flagge of Defiance to their Mischiuous Exercise, and Ouerthrowing their Bulwarkes, by Prophane Writers, Naturall Reason and Common Experience. A Discourse as Pleasaunt for Gentleman that Favors Learning, as Profitable for All that will follow Virtue.*

32. My understanding of this "ongoing effort" derives from the argument developed by Paul Yachnin, *Stage-Wrights: Shakespeare, Jonson, Middleton, and the Making of Theatrical Value* (Philadelphia: University of Pennsylvania Press, 1997).

33. Of course, according to how he frames himself for the audience, Autolycus is in fact a con artist and thief merely *pretending* to be a balladeer. I suggest that this subtle distinction would have made very little difference to Shakespeare's audience: as noted, balladeers were already very closely associated with con artists and thieves in the public imagination. Furthermore, Autolycus has actual ballads for sale, and, according to the servant, he can perform them with a great deal of skill. For all intents and purposes, he *is* a balladeer, regardless of whatever else he might be.

34. Pitcher, ed., *The Winter's Tale*, 388–89.

35. For example, see 2.1.13–14, 2.1.150–52, 4.4.674–78, and 4.4.737.

36. See the essays by Schalkwyk and Lamb for more detailed considerations of women's narratives in *The Winter's Tale*: David Schalkwyk, "A Lady's 'Verily' Is as Potent as a Lord's: Women, Word and Witchcraft in *The Winter's Tale*," *English Literary Renaissance* 22, no. 2 (1992): 242–72; and Mary Ellen Lamb, "Engendering the Narrative Act: Old Wives' Tales in *The Winter's Tale, Macbeth*, and *The Tempest*," *Criticism* 40 (1998): 529–55.

37. The "monstrous birth" story is probably best understood as a subgenre of the prodigy story. Such literature typically projected value onto lurid or strange events by framing them as significations of a divine or vaguely instructional nature. For an excellent overview of the monstrous birth genre, see Cressy, chapter 2: "Monstrous Births and Credible Reports: Portents, Texts, and Testimonies," in *Travesties and Transgressions in Tudor and Stuart England: Tales of Discord and Dissension* (Oxford: Oxford University Press, 2000). Würzbach, *Rise of the English Street Ballad*, discusses monstrous births and prodigies in chapter 4: "Sub-genres of the Street Ballad."

38. Pitcher, ed., *The Winter's Tale*, 142n, notes that "Mopsy" was "a pet name for a lower-class girl," and "Mopsa" was "the name of a stupid country girl mocked by superiors in Sir Phillip Sidney's *New Arcadia*."

39. Cressy, *Travesties and Transgressions*, 46–47.

40. For authentication and interpretation of prodigy stories in ballads and pamphlets, see Cressy, *Travesties and Transgressions*, chapter 2; Raymond, *Pamphlets and Pamphleteering*, 108–22; Aaron Kitch, "Bastards and Broadsides in *The Winter's Tale*," *Renaissance Drama* 30 (1999/2001): 56–57; Würzbach, *Rise of the English Street Ballad*, chapter 4; Sandra Clark, *The Elizabethan Pamphleteers* (London: Athlone Press, 1982), chapter 2; Shaaber, *Some Forerunners*, 204–11; and Jerome Friedman, *The Battle of the Frogs and Fairford's Flies: Miracles and the Pulp Press during the English Revolution* (New York: St. Martin's Press, 1993), chapters 2, 3, 4, and 11.

41. *Strange nevves out of Kent of a monstrous and misshapen child, borne in Olde Sandwitch, vpon the 10. of Iulie, last, the like (for strangenes) hath neuer beene seene* (London, 1609), 3.

42. Ibid. For more on the authentication structure in *Strange Nevves Out of Kent*, see Cressy, *Travesties and Transgressions*, 48.

43. Ibid., 8.

44. Ibid., 11.

45. I do not mean to suggest, however, that stories about strange fish were in any way uncommon throughout the period—quite the opposite, in fact. For example, Pafford notes a 1604 ballad about a half-woman, half-fish in his edition of *The Winter's Tale* (1.2.179, 5.1.102); Würzbach and Fleck discuss other ballad and newsbook reports about gigantic, beached whales (Würzbach, *Rise of the English Street Ballad,* 158–61; Fleck, "Vulgar Fingers of the Multitude," 93–95). See also Cressy, *Travesties and Transgressions,* chapter 2, which discusses other fish stories as well as exhibitions of marvels.

46. A key difference, of course, is that the significance presumed by Autolycus and his audience is of an instructive, rather than divine, nature. I suggest that this distinction should not weigh too heavily, however, given the reticence of commercial drama—especially Shakespearean drama—to present anything that might appear to critique religion or religious belief.

47. Orgel, ed., *The Winter's Tale,* 50.

48. Stanley Cavell, *Disowning Knowledge in Seven Plays of Shakespeare* (Cambridge: Cambridge University Press, 2003), 85.

49. Ibid., 81.

50. Another factor that throws the backstory for the oracular proclamation into doubt is the inconsistent testimony of Cleomenes and Dion: they claim to have heard the "ear-deafening voice" of the priestess as she spoke the proclamation aloud (3.1.8–11), but also claim to have no knowledge of what the written transcript of the proclamation might say (3.1.17–22).

51. There are a number of hints throughout the final act that Paulina's story is a fabrication; see Draper's introduction to Ronald P. Draper, ed., *The Winter's Tale* (Houndmills: Macmillan, 1985): "[we] believe and disbelieve simultaneously, yielding to the theatrical experience . . . and yet [knowing] that what [we] witness is 'romance', that this is not real" (72).

52. On this point see especially Paul Yachnin, "The Perfection of Ten: Populuxe Art and Artisanal Value in *Troilus and Cressida,*" *English Literary Renaissance* 21, no. 1 (1991): 49–74. In contrast to the more philosophically oriented arguments of Lars Engle and Hugh Grady, Yachnin offers a historical analysis that characterizes Shakespeare's antifoundationalism as a corollary to the communitarian, artisanal ethos implicitly promoted by theatrical value-making: Lars Engle, *Shakespearean Pragmatism: Market of His Time* (Chicago: University of Chicago Press, 1993).

53. Engle, *Shakespearean Pragmatism,* 2.

54. Ibid., 9.

55. Ibid., 28, 32, 32.

56. Ibid., 157, 7.

57. For other critical assessments of the Chorus's speech, see L. G. Salinger, "Time and Art in Shakespeare's Romances," *Renaissance Drama* 9 (1966): 3–35; Inga-Stina Ewbank, "The Triumph of Time in *The Winter's Tale,*" *Review of English Literature* 5 (1964): 83–100; and Marion Wells, "Mistress Taleporter and the Triumph of Time: Slander and Old Wives' Tales in *The Winter's Tale,*" *Shakespeare Survey* 58 (2005): 247–59. Of particular note is the connection Wells makes to the popular motto *Temporis filia veritas* (Truth is the daughter of time), and the corresponding idea that time will ultimately uncover (an idealized, Platonic) truth. My argument suggests that Shakespeare offers a new twist on this old idea: time reveals truth, not because truth is

absolute and unavoidable, but because the property "true" derives from an ongoing, temporal process of maintaining a mutable consensus.

58. Note, however, that Ulysses's speech also asserts a (less obvious) endorsement of theatrical value-making. See Yachnin, "'The Perfection of Ten,'" 323.

Chapter 3

1. Gurr estimates that the average weekly attendance rate for London's theaters was somewhere around 2,500: *Playgoing in Shakespeare's London*, 4.

2. Lake and Questier, *The Antichrist's Lewd Hat*, xxxi.

3. See especially T. H. Howard-Hill, *Middleton's "Vulgar Pasquin": Essays on "A Game at Chess"* (Newark: University of Delaware Press, 1995).

4. I use "transposition" to refer to processes by which narratives, ideas, tropes, etc. travel across disparate platforms and change, appear from new angles of view, or take on new meanings as a result of remediation. "Concatenation" refers to a related process of transformation deriving from the combination, or networking, of cultural materials.

5. For an entirely different application of public sphere theory to *Game*, see Ian Munro, "Making Publics: Secrecy and Publication in *A Game at Chess*," *Medieval and Renaissance Drama in England* 14 (2001): 207–26. In contrast to my analysis, Munro argues that an early modern public sphere did in fact exist, and that Middleton's "obvious goal" in *Game* was to counter restrictions on anti-Spanish speech "by speaking out against the Spanish" and "reestablishing a public sphere that [had] been suppressed" (207). See also the analysis of *Game* in Yachnin, "Playing with Space: Making A Public in Middleton's Theatre," in *The Oxford Handbook of Thomas Middleton*, ed. Gary Taylor and Trish T. Henley (Oxford: Oxford University Press, 2012), 32–46, which offers an application of public sphere theory that is much closer to my own argument, but focuses primarily on the capacity of theater to produce new "ideas and experiences of spatiality" (32).

6. Warner, *Publics and Counterpublics*, 62–63.

7. The key source for the surmisal is Dahl, *Bibliography of English Corantos.*

8. See Bellany, *Politics of Court Scandal.*

9. See John Jowett, Introduction to "Measure for Measure," in *Thomas Middleton: The Collected Works* (Oxford: Clarendon, 2007), 1542–46, where Jowett argues that Middleton's revision of the play involved significant transpositions from news discourse surrounding the Thirty Years' War (1544–45).

10. See Bellany, *Politics of Court Scandal.*

11. In addition, see Yachnin's section on *The Witch* in Anthony Dawson and Paul Yachnin, *The Culture of Playgoing in Shakespeare's England: A Collaborative Debate* (Cambridge: Cambridge University Press, 2001), 49–57.

12. There is also at least one direct reference to Frances Howard in *The Changeling*—perhaps more. The best analysis on this material is Annabel Patterson's introduction to the play in *Thomas Middleton: The Collected Works* (Oxford: Clarendon, 2007), 1632–36. See also J. L. Simmons, "Diabolical Realism in Middleton and Rowley's *The Changeling*," *Renaissance Drama* 11 (1980): 135–70; and Christina Malcolmson, "'As Tame as the Ladies': Politics and Gender in *The Changeling*," *English Literary Renaissance* 20, no. 2 (1990): 320–39.

13. *Mistress Turner's Farewell to All Women* may have also inspired the title for Mid-

dleton's *Women Beware Women*. See John Jowett's introduction to "Women Beware Women" in *Thomas Middleton: The Collected Works* (Oxford: Clarendon, 2007), 1489.

14. See Redworth for a full historical account of Charles' trip to Spain: Glyn Redworth, *The Prince and the Infanta: The Cultural Politics of the Spanish Match* (New Haven: Yale University Press, 2003).

15. Thomas Cogswell, "Thomas Middleton and the Court, 1624: *A Game at Chess* in Context," *Huntington Library Quarterly* 47 (1984): 283–84.

16. Bellany, *Politics of Court Scandal*, 176.

17. Yachnin, *Stage-Wrights*, 12.

18. John Holles, "7. John Holles, Lord Haughton to the Earl of Somerset, Wednesday 11 August 1624," in *A Game at Chess*, ed. T. H. Howard-Hill (Manchester: Manchester University Press, 1993), 198–200.

19. Amergio Salvetti, "11. Amergio Salvetti, Florentine Ambassador, to Picchena, Friday [13] 23 August 1624," in Howard-Hill, ed., *A Game at Chess*, 201.

20. Alvise Valaresso, "19. Alvise Valaresso, Venetian Ambassador, to the Doge and Senate, Friday [20] 30 August 1624," in Howard-Hill, ed., *A Game at Chess*, 204.

21. R. A. Davies and A. R. Young, "Strange Cunning in Thomas Middleton's *A Game at Chess*," *University of Toronto Quarterly* 45 (1976): 239. Gary Taylor makes a similar observation in the introduction to his edition of *Game*: "*A Game at Chesse:* A Later Form," in Thomas Middleton, *The Collected Works*, ed. Gary Taylor and John Lavagnino (Oxford: Clarendon, 2007), 1827.

22. All line references and quotations from *Game* correspond to T. H. Howard-Hill's edition of the Trinity manuscript for the Malone Society: T. H. Howard-Hill, ed., *A Game at Chess: 1624* (Oxford: Malone Society, 1990).

23. See Davies and Young, "Strange Cunning," 240; and Cogswell, "Thomas Middleton and the Court," 277.

24. Taylor, "*A Game at Chesse*: An Early Form," in Middleton, *The Collected Works*. Taylor points out that the White King's Pawn recalls the "disgrace of several high officials to whom King James had shown extraordinary favour: the Earl of Somerset (royal favourite, 1615, for murder), the Earl of Suffolk (Lord Treasurer, 1619, for corruption), Sir Francis Bacon (Lord Chancellor, 1621, for bribery), the Earl of Middlesex (Lord Treasurer, 1624, for corruption), and the Earl of Bristol (longtime ambassador to Spain, 1624, for treason)" (1805 n. 224).

25. Richard Dutton, "Receiving Offense: *A Game at Chess* Again," in *Literature and Censorship in Renaissance England*, ed. Andrew Hadfield (New York: Palgrave, 2001), 63.

26. Ibid.

27. See *Macbeth* 1.4.12–15. The similarity between Duncan and the White King may or may not be intentional. Middleton knew *Macbeth* well, having revised it for the King's Men in 1616 (a year, incidentally, when the representation of a weak king would have inevitably drawn comparisons to James). It is therefore not too much of a stretch to suppose that he had Shakespeare's scenography in mind when he wrote these lines. On a related note, a number of critics have noted a similar connection between Malcolm's deception of Macduff in *Macbeth* 4.3 and the White Knight's deception of the Black Knight in *Game* 5.3.

28. Bellany, *Politics of Court Scandal*, 254–55, 258.

29. The Black Jesting Pawn speaks this line when he finds himself at the front of a chain of three pawns simultaneously "firking" each other from behind.

30. The Black Knight makes this joke as he reads through the Fat Bishop's book listing the price of pardons for various sins.

31. The Black Knight makes this joke as he examines a letter written in Italian. "The Hebrew way" refers to Hebrew script, which goes from right to left, rather than left to right, and is thus "backwards." The joke, then, is that Italian writers put their "pens" (penises) in "backwards," a reference to anal intercourse. See Richard Dutton, ed., *A Game at Chess*, in Thomas Middleton, *"Women Beware Women" and Other Plays* (Oxford: Oxford University Press, 1999), 422 n. 301.

32. Dutton, "Receiving Offense," 68.

33. Bellany, *Politics of Court Scandal*, 255–57, 255.

34. Margot Heinemann, *Puritanism and Theatre: Thomas Middleton and Opposition Drama under the Early Stuarts* (Cambridge: Cambridge University Press, 1980), 164.

35. Elena Levy-Navarro, *The Culture of Obesity in Early and Late Modernity: Body Image in Shakespeare, Jonson, Middleton, and Skelton* (New York: Palgrave Macmillan, 2008), 138.

36. See Howard-Hill, *Middleton's "Vulgar Pasquin"*, 107, and Cogswell, "Thomas Middleton and the Court," 279.

37. In this extract, "Mel Aerium" means "a nourishing source of amusement."

38. Howard-Hill, *Middleton's "Vulgar Pasquin"*, 237–52.

39. Ibid.

40. See P. G. Lake, "Constitutional Consensus and Puritan Opposition in the 1620s: Thomas Scott and the Spanish Match," *Historical Journal* 25, no. 4 (1982): 823, 818.

41. Scott discusses the influence of the theatre on his style in *Vox Populi, or Newes from Spayne* (London, 1620): "Might I not borrow a Spanish name or two to grace this Comedie with stately actors? Or must they onely be reserved for Kingly Tragedies? Why not Gondomar as well as Hieronymo Duke D'Alva?" (10).

42. Alexander Samson, "1623 and the Politics of Translation," in *The Spanish Match: Prince Charles' Journey to Madrid, 1623*, ed. Alexander Samson (London: Ashgate, 2006), 106.

43. See Yachnin, "The Perfection of Ten." The portmanteau "populuxe" describes "popular versions of deluxe material and cultural goods or elite comportment or aristocratic forms of recreation." Yachnin writes that the "populuxe theatre . . . created a theatrical culture of emulation and masquerade that drew ordinary Londoners to the playhouse where they could drink in ersatz versions of courtly entertainment and could even hear something of court news" (86).

44. My understanding of the Hispanophilia reflected in *Game* owes a great deal to Trudi Darby's essay "The Black Knight's Festival Book? Thomas Middleton's *A Game at Chess*," in Samson, *The Spanish Match*, 173–88. Although I find Darby's argument connecting the play to festival literature too reductive, her analysis of an "ambiguous image of Spain as grudgingly admired and loathed" provided the inspiration for this section (Alexander Samson, "Introduction: The Spanish Match," in Samson, *The Spanish Match*, 6). For more on representations of Spain in *Game*, see Barbara Fuchs, "Middleton and Spain," in Trish and Henley, *Oxford Handbook of Thomas Middleton*, 404–17, and Eric Griffin, *English Renaissance Drama and the Specter of Spain* (Philadelphia: University of Pennsylvania Press, 2009).

45. Taylor, "*A Game at Chesse*: An Early Form," 1817 n. 38.

46. Howard-Hill, ed., *A Game at Chess*, 170 n. 45.

47. John Chamberlain, *The Letters of John Chamberlain*, ed. Norman McClure

(Philadelphia: American Philosophical Society, 1939), 2.391. Chamberlain records a noteworthy example in a letter to Sir Dudley Carleton of 21 July 1621, which notes a high-profile appearance by Gondomar at the Fortune Theatre.

48. Editors disagree on this point. Chamberlain's letter of 21 August states that the players "had gotten (they say) a cast sute of [Gondomar's] apparell for the purpose, with his Lytter." As Chamberlain points out, his knowledge of the provenance of the suit and litter derived from hearsay. Richard Dutton takes the rumor as fact (ibid., xxxi), as does Gary Taylor ("*A Game at Chesse*: An Early Form," 1775). Howard-Hill, *Middleton's "Vulgar Pasquin"*, notes that "the players need not have acquired Gondomar's own accouterments . . . any chair of ease and litter would have served (128 n. 23).

49. Howard-Hill, *Middleton's "Vulgar Pasquin"*, 237–52.

50. See Woolley, "6. John Woolley to William Trumbull, Wednesday 11 August," in Howard-Hill, ed., *A Game at Chess*, 198; and Chamberlain, "21. John Chamberlain to Sir Dudley Carleton, Saturday 21 August 1624," in Howard-Hill, ed., *A Game at Chess*, 205. In his letter of 20 August, Woolley also refers to the play more succinctly as "Gundomar": "17. John Woolley to William Trumbull, Friday 20 August 1624," in Howard-Hill, ed., *A Game at Chess*, 203.

51. Don Carlos Coloma, "5. Don Carlos Coloma to the Conde-Duque Olivares, Tuesday [10] 20 August 1624," in Howard-Hill, ed., *A Game at Chess*, 194–95.

52. Salvetti, "Amergio Salvetti, Florentine Ambassador, to Picchena," 201.

53. Francis Nethersole, "13. Sir Francis Nethersole to Sir Dudley Carleton, Saturday 14 August 1624," in Howard-Hill, ed., *A Game at Chess*, 202.

54. Woolley, "2. John Woolley to William Trumbull, Friday 6 August 1624," in Howard-Hill, ed., *A Game at Chess*, 192–93.

55. Ibid., 198.

56. Dutton, "Receiving Offense," 53–54.

57. Paul L. Hughes and James F. Larkin, eds., *Tudor Royal Proclamations* (New Haven: Yale University Press 1969), 2.496.

58. See Dutton, "Receiving Offense," for analysis of the delicate diplomatic maneuvering around *Game*.

59. The leniency accorded to the players has led critics such as Heinemann and Limon to conclude that the play must have had a powerful protector at court: Heinemann, *Puritanism and Theatre*; Jerzy Limon, *Dangerous Matter: English Drama and Politics in 1623–24* (Cambridge: Cambridge University Press, 1986). In "Receiving Offense," Richard Dutton provides a powerful refutation of such theories. His analysis of the political situation at the time and the practices of the Master of the Revels suggests that officials did not regard *Game* (a mere play) as an object worthy of serious indignation. He argues that officials only shut the production down to placate the new Spanish ambassador, Don Carlos Coloma, and had no motivation to punish the players any further.

60. Chamberlain, "John Chamberlain to Sir Dudley Carleton," 205.

61. Ibid.

Chapter 4

1. See Mark Z. Muggli, "Ben Jonson and the Business of News," *SEL* 32, no. 2 (1992): 323–40, for a more detailed discussion of news throughout the Jonsonian corpus.

2. All quotes and line references pertaining to Jonson are from *The Cambridge Edition of the Works of Ben Jonson*, ed. David M. Bevington, Martin Butler, and Ian Donaldson (Cambridge: Cambridge University Press, 2012).

3. See chapter 2 for a discussion of the mock ballads in *The Winter's Tale* and the relation of balladry to early seventeenth-century news culture.

4. Note that the term "newsmonger" suggests that these individuals are not merely passive consumers of news, but are also actively caught up in a process of informal distribution.

5. The report is doubly portentous because it combines two harbingers of ill omen: ravens and birds' nests on boats.

6. For a discussion of prodigy narratives in news, see chapter 2.

7. Jonson refers to a popular fantasy that Spinola, a renowned inventor of war machines, had a whale that would swim up the Thames and drown all of London by blowing water out of its spout. A similar joke occurs in *Staple* 3.2.41–42.

8. Most news of international events came to England via the Low Countries. See Folke Dahl, "Amsterdam—Cradle of English Newspapers," *The Library*, 5th ser. 4, no. 3 (1949): 166–78; and Fleck, "Vulgar Fingers of the Multitude."

9. See 2.1.94, 2.3.13, and 4.1.52.

10. See Love, *Scribal Publication*, 35–89, on rhetorical uses of medium to connote exclusivity or publicity, often in defiance of practice.

11. Gazettes were commercially sold, inexpensive, handwritten newssheets that began to appear in Italy around 1650. They provided the basic model for the printed news products, such as corantos, that became popular in the seventeenth century. See Mitchell Stephens, *A History of News: From the Drum to the Satellite* (New York: Viking, 1988), 149–55.

12. For a discussion of *Mercurius Gallobelgicus*, see chapter 2.

13. See Lauren Shohet, *Reading Masques: The English Masque and Public Culture in the Seventeenth Century* (Oxford: Oxford University Press, 2010), 178–80.

14. As noted in chapter 1, the categorical difference between "history" and "news" was much less distinct in the early seventeenth century than it is today. See Woolf, "News, History, and the Construction," 98: "The corantos and early newsbooks of the 1620s speak of news as history and often were published under the rubric of history, a further reinforcement of the argument that at its earliest stage the published news was perceived as a record of the recent past, not of an ongoing present."

15. Note that Jonson reuses this exchange in *Staple* 1.5.42–54.

16. See chapter 2 for a discussion of attitudes toward truth and print in *The Winter's Tale* 4.4.

17. Jonson is likely assuming a connection between delight and education—as in Horace and Sidney, for example.

18. Both quotations from Warner, *Publics and Counterpublics*, 71.

19. D. F. McKenzie, "*The Staple of News* and the Late Plays," in *A Celebration of Ben Jonson*, ed. William Blisset, Julian Patrick, and R. W. van Fossen (Toronto: University of Toronto Press, 1972), 92.

20. Ibid.

21. On the Blackfriars' audience, see Andrew Gurr, "London's Blackfriars Playhouse and the Chamberlain's Men," in *Inside Shakespeare: Essays on the Blackfriars Stage*, ed. Paul Menzer (Selinsgrove: Susquehanna University Press, 2006), 17.

22. Parr, ed., *The Staple of News*, 67 n. 53.

23. Stuart Sherman, "Eyes and Ears, News, and Plays: The Argument of Ben Jonson's *Staple*," in Dooley and Baron, *Politics of Information*, 30.

24. The proliferation of paratextual material in the play is unusual for printed playtexts, but not so unusual for printed masques.

25. On Jonson and authorial self-construction, see Joseph Loewenstein, *Ben Jonson and Possessive Authorship* (Cambridge: Cambridge University Press, 2002), 133–210; for Jonson and marginalia, see Evelyn Tribble, "Genius on the Rack: Authorities and the Margin in Ben Jonson's Glossed Works," *Exemplaria* 4, no. 2 (1992): 317–39, and Stephen Orgel, "Marginal Jonson," in *The Politics of the Stuart Court Masque*, ed. David Bevington and Peter Holbrook (Cambridge: Cambridge University Press, 1998), 144–75.

26. See Yachnin, "The Perfection of Ten," 86.

27. Note that Jonson satirizes the consumers of manuscript news for buying into a similar illusion of exclusive belonging. See my analysis of *Volpone* and *News from the New World Discovered in the Moon.*

28. Parr, ed., *The Staple of News,* 71 n. 8.

29. See chapter 3 for a discussion of visual parallels between *The Second Part of Vox Populi* and *A Game at Chess.*

30. Jonson's eagerness to distance himself from cheap print may have also contributed to his motivation for the anomalous authorial project of publishing his *Workes* (London, 1616). See Loewenstein, *Ben Jonson and Possessive Authorship,* 133–210.

31. *Ficta . . . veris.* This is a quotation from *Horace's Art of Poetry.* In *Epicoene, or, The Silent Woman* Jonson translates it as "Poet never credit gain'd / By writing truths, but things (like truths) well fain'd" (Second Prologue, 9–10) (Parr, ed., *The Staple of News,* n. 153). Note that Jonson makes the exact same point at the conclusion of *News from the New World Discovered in the Moon.*

32. Sherman, "Eyes and Ears," 35.

33. For example, see Fleck, "Vulgar Fingers of the Multitude," 87, and Julie Sanders, "Print, Popular Culture, Consumption and Commodification in *The Staple of News,*" in *Refashioning Ben Jonson: Gender, Politics, and the Jonsonian Canon,* ed. Julie Sanders, Kate Chedgzoy, and Susan Wiseman (New York: St. Martin's Press, 1998), 183.

34. McKenzie, "*The Staple of News* and the Late Plays," 107.

35. Ibid.

36. Dawson and Yachnin, *Culture of Playgoing,* 194. As Yachnin notes, the reporters and clerks who work at the Staple are also sharers in the business, an organizational structure that "resembles nothing quite so much as the King's Servants system of sharers."

37. As noted in regard to *News from the New World Discovered in the Moon,* this variety of categories suggests a cynical disregard for ideological commitment on the part of commercial news.

38. For Gainsford, see chapter 1.

39. Parr, ed., *The Staple of News,* 116 n. 60.

40. Muggli, "Ben Jonson and the Business of News," 336.

41. Parr, ed., *The Staple of News,* 26–29.

42. "The thirtieth of February" is, of course, a calendric impossibility. Shakespeare makes a similar joke in the singing fish ballad from the *Winter's Tale,* which recounts an event that supposedly took place on "the fourscore of April," or April eightieth (4.4.276). See chapter 2.

43. Spinola was one of the most talked-about figures in news of the Thirty Years' War, and had a reputation as an inventor of war machines. Jonson composed a similar mock report about the general twenty years earlier for *Volpone* (2.1.50–51).

44. The Anabaptists were a radical Protestant sect known for their belief in adult baptism.

45. Turkey was a key foe of the Protestant cause in the Thirty Years' War, and features prominently in news discourse of the time; see chapter 1.

46. For further discussion of this story, see chapter 3.

47. The title pages of newsbooks typically listed summaries of the reports they conveyed, putting particular emphasis on the names of famous newsmakers.

48. "House of Fame" is also a specific reference Chaucer's poem of the same name. Shakespeare makes a similar connection between *fama* and news in the induction to 2 *Henry IV.* See chapter 2.

49. For example, see Fleck, "Vulgar Fingers of the Multitude," 107–8 and Muggli, "Ben Jonson and the Business of News," 332.

50. Dawson and Yachnin, *Culture of Playgoing,* 195–96. See chapter 8 ("The House of Fame"), in which Yachnin discusses the populuxe orientation of the early modern theater, drawing on examples from both *The Staple of News* and *A Game at Chess.*

51. Dawson and Yachnin, *Culture of Playgoing,* 55.

Epilogue

1. Andrew Pettegree, *The Invention of News: How the World Came to Know about Itself* (New Haven: Yale University Press, 2014), 372.

Bibliography

Critical Editions

Bevington, David, ed. *The Complete Works of Shakespeare.* 6th edition. New York: Pearson Longman, 2006.

Bevington, David, Martin Butler, and Ian Donaldson, eds. *The Cambridge Edition of the Works of Ben Jonson.* Cambridge: Cambridge University Press, 2012.

Dutton, Richard, ed. *A Game at Chess.* In Thomas Middleton, *"Women Beware Women" and Other Plays.* Oxford: Oxford University Press, 1999. 237–316.

Draper, Ronald P., ed. *The Winter's Tale.* Houndmills: Macmillan, 1985.

Howard-Hill, T. H., ed. *A Game at Chess.* Manchester: Manchester University Press, 1993.

Howard-Hill, T. H., ed. *A Game at Chess: 1624.* Oxford: Malone Society, 1990.

Orgel, Stephen, ed. *The Winter's Tale.* New York: Oxford University Press, 1998.

Pafford, John H. P., ed. *The Winter's Tale.* London: Methuen, 1963.

Parr, Anthony, ed. *The Staple of News.* Manchester: Manchester University Press, 1999.

Pitcher, John, ed. *The Winter's Tale.* London: Arden Shakespeare, 2010.

Snyder, Susan, and Deborah T. Curren-Aquino, eds. *The Winter's Tale.* Cambridge: Cambridge University Press, 2007.

Tatspaugh, Patricia, ed. *The Winter's Tale.* London: Arden Shakespeare, 2002.

Taylor, Gary, ed. "*A Game at Chess:* A Later Form." In *Thomas Middleton: The Collected Works.* Edited by Gary Taylor and John Lavagnino. Oxford: Clarendon Press, 2007. 1825–85.

Taylor, Gary. "*A Game at Chesse:* An Early Form." In *Thomas Middleton: The Collected Works.* Edited by Gary Taylor and John Lavagnino. Oxford: Oxford University Press, 2007. 1773–1824.

Contemporary Documents

Anonymous newsletter of 8 August 1628. Isham of Lamport Manuscript Collection, Northamptonshire Record Office (NRO), MS IL 2671, fol. 1v.

Anonymous newsletter of 8 August 1628. Isham of Lamport MSS, NRO MS IL 2671, fol. 2r.

Chamberlain, John. "21. John Chamberlain to Sir Dudley Carleton, Saturday 21 August 1624." In *A Game at Chess.* Edited by T. H. Howard-Hill. Manchester: Manchester University Press, 1993. 205.

Coloma, Don Carlos. "4. Don Carlos Coloma to James I, Saturday [7] 17 August 1624." In *A Game at Chess.* Edited by T. H. Howard-Hill. Manchester: Manchester University Press, 1993. 193–94.

Coloma, Don Carlos. "5. Don Carlos Coloma to the Conde-Duque Olivares, Tuesday [10] 20 August 1624." In *A Game at Chess.* Edited by T. H. Howard-Hill. Manchester: Manchester University Press, 1993. 194–98.

Coloma, Don Carlos. "15. Don Carlos Coloma to the Conde-Duque Olivares, Wednesday [18] 28 August 1624." In *A Game at Chess.* Edited by T. H. Howard-Hill. Manchester: Manchester University Press, 1993. 202–3.

Conway, Edward. "8. Sir Edward Conway, Secretary of State, to the Privy Council, Thursday 12 August 1624." In *A Game at Chess.* Edited by T. H. Howard-Hill. Manchester: Manchester University Press, 1993. 200.

Conway, Edward. "9. Sir Edward Conway to Don Carlos Coloma, Undated; [Probably 12 August 1624]." In *A Game at Chess.* Edited by T. H. Howard-Hill. Manchester: Manchester University Press, 1993. 200–201.

Conway, Edward. "22. Sir Edward Conway, Secretary of State, to the Privy Council, Friday 27 August 1624." In *A Game at Chess.* Edited by T. H. Howard-Hill. Manchester: Manchester University Press, 1993. 206.

Herbert, William. "23. The Earl of Pembroke, Lord Chamberlain, to the President of the Council, Viscount Mandeville, Friday 27 August 1624." In *A Game at Chess.* Edited by T. H. Howard-Hill. Manchester: Manchester University Press, 1993. 206–7.

Holles, John. "7. John Holles, Lord Haughton to the Earl of Somerset, Wednesday 11 August 1624." In *A Game at Chess.* Edited by T. H. Howard-Hill. Manchester: Manchester University Press, 1993. 198–200.

Holles, John. "30. Inscription in Copy of Second Quarto, 1625." In *A Game at Chess.* Edited by T. H. Howard-Hill. Manchester: Manchester University Press, 1993. 211.

Lowe, George. "3. George Lowe to Sir Arthur Ingram, Saturday 7 August 1624." In *A Game at Chess.* Edited by T. H. Howard-Hill. Manchester: Manchester University Press, 1993. 193.

Lowe, George. "1. Master of the Revels's License, 12 June 1624." In *A Game at Chess.* Edited by T. H. Howard-Hill. Manchester: Manchester University Press, 1993. 192.

Nethersole, Francis. "13. Sir Francis Nethersole to Sir Dudley Carleton, Saturday 14 August 1624." In *A Game at Chess.* Edited by T. H. Howard-Hill. Manchester: Manchester University Press, 1993. 202.

Nethersole, Francis. "16. Sir Francis Nethersole to Sir Dudley Carleton, Thursday 19 August 1624." In *A Game at Chess.* Edited by T. H. Howard-Hill. Manchester: Manchester University Press, 1993. 203.

Overton, Paul. "10. Paul Overton to Dr. William Bishop, Bishop of Chalcedon, Friday [13] 23 [August] 1624." In *A Game at Chess.* Edited by T. H. Howard-Hill. Manchester: Manchester University Press, 1993. 201.

Privy Council. "14. Privy Council, Wednesday 18 August 1624." In *A Game at Chess.* Edited by T. H. Howard-Hill. Manchester: Manchester University Press, 1993. 202.

Privy Council. "20. Privy Council to Sir Edward Conway, Saturday 21 August 1624." In *A Game at Chess.* Edited by T. H. Howard-Hill. Manchester: Manchester University Press, 1993. 204.

Privy Council. "26. Privy Council, Monday 30 August 1624." In *A Game at Chess.* Edited by T. H. Howard-Hill. Manchester: Manchester University Press, 1993. 207.

Privy Council. "27. Privy Council, Monday 30 August 1624." In *A Game at Chess.* Edited by T. H. Howard-Hill. Manchester: Manchester University Press, 1993. 208.

Salisbury, Thomas. "28. Thomas Salisbury in Sir Thomas Dawe's Commonplace Book, 1 December 1624." In *A Game at Chess.* Edited by T. H. Howard-Hill. Manchester: Manchester University Press, 1993. 208–10.

Salvetti, Amergio. "11. Amergio Salvetti, Florentine Ambassador, to Picchena, Friday [13] 23 August 1624." In *A Game at Chess.* Edited by T. H. Howard-Hill. Manchester: Manchester University Press, 1993. 201.

Salvetti, Amergio. "12. Amergio Salvetti, Florentine Ambassador, to Sir John Scudamore, Bart., Saturday 14 August 1624." In *A Game at Chess.* Edited by T. H. Howard-Hill. Manchester: Manchester University Press, 1993. 202.

Salvetti, Amergio. "18. Amergio Salvetti, Florentine Ambassador, to The Secretary, Friday [20] 30 August 1624." In *A Game at Chess.* Edited by T. H. Howard-Hill. Manchester: Manchester University Press, 1993. 203.

Salvetti, Amergio. "31. Sir Thomas Dawes's Commonplace Book, 1624–8." In *A Game at Chess.* Edited by T. H. Howard-Hill. Manchester: Manchester University Press, 1993. 211–12.

Valaresso, Alvise. "19. Alvise Valaresso, Venetian Ambassador, to the Doge and Senate, Friday [20] 30 August 1624." In *A Game at Chess.* Edited by T. H. Howard-Hill. Manchester: Manchester University Press, 1993. 204.

Valaresso, Alvise. "24. Alvise Valaresso, Venetian Ambassador, to the Doge and Senate, Friday [27 August] 6 September 1624." In *A Game at Chess.* Edited by T. H. Howard-Hill. Manchester: Manchester University Press, 1993. 207.

Woolley, John. "2. John Woolley to William Trumbull, Friday 6 August 1624." In *A Game at Chess.* Edited by T. H. Howard-Hill. Manchester: Manchester University Press, 1993. 192–93.

Woolley, John. "6. John Woolley to William Trumbull, Wednesday 11 August." In *A Game at Chess.* Edited by T. H. Howard-Hill. Manchester: Manchester University Press, 1993. 198.

Woolley, John. "17. John Woolley to William Trumbull, Friday 20 August 1624." In *A Game at Chess.* Edited by T. H. Howard-Hill. Manchester: Manchester University Press, 1993. 203.

Woolley, John. "25. John Woolley to William Trumbull, Saturday 28 August 1624." In *A Game at Chess.* Edited by T. H. Howard-Hill. Manchester: Manchester University Press, 1993. 207.

Contemporary Publications

The Affaires of Italy, with the Crowning and Inauguration of the New Pope Barbarino a Florentine in Rome, and Other Accidents. London, 1623.

Almansa y Mendoza, Andrés de. *The Joyful Return of the Most Illustrious Prince Charles, Prince of Great Britain, from the Court of Spain.* London, 1623.

Almansa y Mendoza, Andrés de. *Two Royall Entertainments, Lately Given to the Most Illustrious Prince Charles at the Feasts of Easter and Pentecost.* London, 1623.

The Arraignment of Iohn van Olden Barneuelt Late Aduocate of Holland and West-Freisland Containing the Articles Alleadged Against Him, and the Reasons of His Execution, Being Performed vpon the 13. of May Anno 1619. London, 1619.

Barnevelt Displayed: or The Golden Legend of New St Iohn; Found Out in the Vnited Prouinces of the Low-Countries. Comprehending a Short Rehearsall of the Noblenesse, Vertues, and Actions of Mr. Iohn of Barnevelt, Late Aduocate and Speaker for the Prouinces of Holland and West-Friesland. London, 1619.

Chamberlain, John. *The Letters of John Chamberlain.* Edited by Norman McClure. Philadelphia: American Philosophical Society, 1939.

The Continuation of Our Newes from the 4. to the 17 of this Instant. London, 1630.

The Continuation of Our Weekely Newes, from the 16 August to the 24 of the Same. London, 1626.

Culverwell, Ezekiel. *A Treatise of Faith Wherein is Declared How a Man May Live by Faith, and Find Relief in all his Necessities.* London, 1623.

Day, John. *Law-Tricks.* London, 1608.

Dekker, Thomas. *The Whore of Babylon.* London, 1607.

Digby, John. *A Continuation of a Former Relation Concerning the Entertainment Given to the Prince his Highness by the King of Spain in his Court at Madrid.* London, 1623.

Digby, John. *A True Relation and Journal of the Manner of Arrival, and Magnificent Entertainment Given to the High and Mighty Prince Charles by the King of Spain in his Court at Madrid.* London, 1623.

Gee, John. *The Foot Out of the Snare: With a Detection of Svndry Late Practices and Impostures of the Priests and Iesuits in England.* London, 1624.

Gee, John. *New Shreds of the Old Snare.* London, 1624.

Goad, Thomas. *The Dolefull Euen-Song.* London, 1623.

Goad, Thomas. *The Friars Chronicle: or, The Trve Legend of Priests and Monkes Lives.* London, 1623.

Granada, Luis de. *F. L. Granada's Meditations, Containing Fourteene Deuout Exercises, For the Seuen Daies of the Weeke. Both for Mornings and Euenings.* Translated by Richard Hopkins. London, 1623.

Greene, Robert. *The Third and Last Part of Conny-Catching. With the new Deuised Knauish Arte of Foole-Taking. The Like Coosnages and Villanies Neuer Before Discouered.* London, 1592.

Heuy Newes of an Horryble Earth Quake whiche was in the Cytie of Scharbaria in this Present Yeare of. XLII. The XIII. Day of June. Also how that a Cytie in Turky is Sonke. London, 1622.

Hieron, Samuel. *The Sermons of Master Samvel Hieron.* London, 1624.

The High and Mighty Prince Charles, Prince of Wales, &c. The Manner of his Arriual at the Spanish Court, the Magnificence of his Royall Entertainment There. London, 1623.

Hockham, William. *Prince Charles His Welcome to the Court, or, A True Subiects Loue for His Happy Returne from Spaine.* London, 1623.

James, Thomas. *The Iesuits Downefall.* Oxford, 1612.

Late Newes or True Relations, 30. London, 1624.

Marston, John. *The Insatiate Countesse.* London, 1613.

Marston, John. *The Malcontent.* London, 1604.

Mercurius Gallobelgicus: Siue, Rerum in Gallia & Belgio Potissimum: Hispania quoque, Italia, Anglia, Germania, Polonia, Vicinisque Locis ab Anno 1588 vsque ad Martium . . . 1594 gestarum, Nuncius. Cologne, 1594.

Micanzio, Fulgenzio. *An Exact and Sound Discovery of the Chiefe Mysteries of Jesuiticall Iniquity.* Translated by Isaac Bargrave. London, 1619.

Middleton, Thomas. *The Phoenix.* London, 1607.

Middleton, Thomas. *A Yorkshire Tragedy.* London, 1608.

Middleton, Thomas, and William Rowley. *The Roaring Girl. Or Moll Cut-Purse.* London, 1611.

More Newes; Containing, the Trovbles in the Empire vpon the Comming of Bethlem Gabor. London, 1623.

Newes From Rome, Spalatto's Doome, or An Epitome of the Life and Behavior of M. Antonius de Dominis. London, 1624.

Newes out of Holland: Concerning Barnevelt and his Fellow-Prisoners their Conspiracy against their Natiue Country, with the Enemies Thereof: The Oration and Propositions Made in Their Behalfe vnto the Generall States of the Vnited Prouinces at the Hagve, by the Ambassadors of the French King. London, 1619.

Pattenson, Matthew. *The Image of Bothe Chvrches, Hiervsalem and Babel, Vnitie and Confvsion, Obedience and Sedition.* Tornay, 1623.

Peña, Juan Antonio de la. *A Relation of the Royall Festiuities, and Juego de Cañas . . . Made by the King of Spaine at Madrid, the 21 of August this Present Yeere, 1623.* London, 1623.

Reynolds, John. *Vox Coeli, or, Newes from Heaven of a Consulation There Held.* London, 1624.

Rivet, André. *The State-Mysteries of the Iesvites, By Way of Questions and Answers.* Translated by Peter Gosselin. London, 1623.

Robinson, Thomas. *The Anatomy of the English Nunnery at Lisbon in Portugall.* London, 1622.

Scott, Thomas. *Englands Ioy, For Svppressing the Papists, and Banishing the Priests and Iesuites.* London, 1624.

Scott, Thomas. *An Experimentall Discoverie of Spanish Practices, or, The Covnsell of a Well-Wishing Souldier, for the Good of His Prince and State.* London, 1623.

Scott, Thomas. *The Proiector Teaching a Direct, Sure, and Ready Way to Restore the Decayes of the Church and State both in Honour and Revenue.* London, 1624.

Scott, Thomas. *Robert Earle of Essex his Ghost, Sent from Elizian to the Nobility, Gentry, and Communaltie of England.* London, 1624.

Scott, Thomas. *The Second Part of Vox Populi, or Gondomar Appearing in the Likenes of a Matchiauell in a Spanish Parliament.* London, 1624.

Scott, Thomas. *Vox Dei.* Holland, 1624.

Scott, Thomas. *Vox Regis.* Utrecht, 1624.

Scott, Thomas. *Vox Populi, or Newes from Spayne.* London, 1620.

Speght, Rachel. *A Mouzell for Melastomus, the Cynicall Bayter of, and Foule Mouthed Barker against Euahs Sex.* London, 1616.

The Strangling and Death of the Great Turke, and his two Sonnes With the Strange Preservation and Deliverance of his Vncle Mustapha from Perishing in Prison, with Hunger and Thirst, the Young Emperour Now Three Dayes before Having so Commanded. London, 1622.

Swetnam, Joseph. *The Araignment of Lewd, Idle, Froward, and Vnconstant Women or, the Vanitie of Them, Choose you Whether.* London, 1615.

The True Description of the Execution of Ivstice, Done in the Grauenhage, by the Counsell of the Generall States Holden for the Same Purpose, vpon Sir Iohn van Olden Barnauelt. Against Whom the Said States Pvrposely therevnto Appointed, did Worthily Pronounce Sentence of Death According to his Deserts; which was Executed vpon the Third Day of May, 1619. London, 1619.

A True Discovery of those Treasons of which Geilis Van Ledenberch was a Practiser Against the Generall States of the Vnited Netherland Prouinces; Through the Aduise, and Assistance of Iohn van Olden Barneuelt. And for which (after Arraignment, Sentence and Iudgement) Execution was Done on the Dead Body of the said Ledenberch, After he had Most Inhumanly Murthered Himselfe, through the Guiltines, and Horror of his Conscience. London, 1619.

A True Relation of that which Lately Hapned to the Great Spanish Fleet, and Galeons of Terra Firma in America. London, 1623.

Webster, John. *The White Devil, or, The tragedy of Paulo Giordano Vrsini, Duke of Brachiano with the Life and Death of Vittoria Corombona the Famous Venetian curtizan.* London, 1612.

Secondary Sources

Adelman, Janet. *The Common Liar: An Essay on "Antony and Cleopatra".* New Haven: Yale University Press, 1973.

Anderson, Benedict. *Imagined Communities: Reflections on the Origin and Spread of Nationalism.* London: Verso, 1991.

Appleton, William W. *Beaumont and Fletcher: A Critical Study.* London: Allen & Unwin, 1956.

Arber, Edward, ed. *A Transcript of the Registers of the Company of Stationers of London: 1554–1640 A.D.* 5 vols. London: Privately Printed, 1875–94.

Atherton, Ian. "The Itch Grown a Disease: Manuscript Transmission of News in the Seventeenth Century." In *News, Newspapers, and Society in Early Modern Britain.* Edited by Joad Raymond. Portland: Frank Cass, 1999. 39–65.

Barfoot, C. C. "News of the Roman Empire: Hearsay, Soothsay, Myth and History in *Antony and Cleopatra.*" In *Reclamations of Shakespeare.* Edited by A. J. Hoenselaars. Amsterdam: Rodopi, 1994. 103–28.

Baron, Sabrina A. "The Guises of Dissemination in Early Seventeenth-Century England." In *The Politics of Information in Early Modern Europe.* Edited by Brendan Dooley and Sabrina A. Baron. London: Routledge, 2001. 41–57.

Bawcutt, N. W. "New Light on Middleton's Knowledge of Chess." *Notes & Queries* 232 (1987): 301–2.

Bawcutt, N. W. "Was Thomas Middleton a Puritan Dramatist?" *Modern Language Review* 94 (1999): 925–39.

Bellany, Alastair. *The Politics of Court Scandal in Early Modern England: News Culture and the Overbury Affair, 1603–1660.* Cambridge: Cambridge University Press, 2002.

Bellany, Alastair. "Raylinge Rymes and Vaunting Verse: Libelous Politics in Early Stuart England, 1603–1628." In *Culture and Politics in Early Stuart England.* Edited by Kevin Sharpe and Peter Lake. Stanford: Stanford University Press, 1993. 285–311.

Bicks, Caroline. "Staging the Jesuitess in *A Game at Chess.*" *SEL* 49 (2009): 463–84.

Bothe, Michael G. "The Puppet and the Priest: Theatrical Ephemera in Early Modern London." Diss. University of Arkansas, Fayetteville, 2003.

Boyce, George, James Curran, and Pauline Wingate. *Newspaper History from the Seventeenth Century to the Present Day*. London: Constable, 1978.

Braunmuller, A. R. "To the Globe I Rowed: John Holles Sees *A Game at Chess*." *English Literary Renaissance* 20 (1990): 340–56.

Brownlees, Nicholas. "Spoken Discourse in Early English Newspapers." In *News Networks in the Seventeenth Century: Britain and Europe*. Edited by Joad Raymond. London: Routledge, 2006. 67–84.

Bullough, Geoffrey. "*The Game at Chesse:* How It Struck a Contemporary." *Modern Language Review* 49 (1954): 156–60.

Butler, Martin. "Jonson's *News from the New World*, the 'Running Masque,' and the Season of 1619–20." *Medieval and Renaissance Drama in England* 6 (1993): 153–67.

Calhoun, Craig J. *Habermas and the Public Sphere*. Cambridge, MA: MIT Press, 1992.

Cavell, Stanley. *Disowning Knowledge in Seven Plays of Shakespeare*. Cambridge: Cambridge University Press, 2003.

Cayley, David. "The Origins of the Modern Public Episode 1: An Introduction to Making Publics and to the Early Modern Period." *Ideas*. CBC. 26 April 2010. *iTunes Podcasts*. Web. 1 September 2010.

Cayley, David. "The Origins of the Modern Public Episode 2: The Reformation." *Ideas*. CBC, 27 April 2010. *iTunes Podcasts*. Web. 1 September 2010.

Cayley, David. "The Origins of the Modern Public Episode 3: Forms of Nationhood." *Ideas*. CBC. 28 April 2010. *iTunes Podcasts*. Web. 1 September 1 2010.

Cayley, David. "The Origins of the Modern Public Episode 4: The Print Revolution." *Ideas*. CBC. 29 April 2010. *iTunes Podcasts*. Web. 1 September 2010.

Cayley, David. "The Origins of the Modern Public Episode 5: Painting Modernity." *Ideas*. CBC. 30 April 2010. *iTunes Podcasts*. Web. 1 September 2010.

Cayley, David. "The Origins of the Modern Public Episode 6: Elizabethan/Jacobean Theatre." *Ideas*. CBC. 5 May 2010. *iTunes Podcasts*. Web. 1 September 2010.

Cayley, David. "The Origins of the Modern Public Episode 7: Theatre and Publics." *Ideas*. CBC. 12 May 2010. *iTunes Podcasts*. Web. 1 September 2010.

Cayley, David. "The Origins of the Modern Public Episode 8: The Private Goes Public." *Ideas*. CBC. 19 May 2010. *iTunes Podcasts*. Web. 1 September 2010.

Cayley, David. "The Origins of the Modern Public Episode 9: The Secret History of Domesticity." *Ideas*. CBC. 26 May. 2010. *iTunes Podcasts*. Web. 1 September 2010.

Cayley, David. "The Origins of the Modern Public Episode 10: Science and Its Publics." *Ideas*. CBC. 2 June 2010. *iTunes Podcasts*. Web. 1 September 2010.

Cayley, David. "The Origins of the Modern Public Episode 11: Steps to a Public Sphere." *Ideas*. CBC. 9 June 2010. *iTunes Podcasts*. Web. 1 September 2010.

Cayley, David. "The Origins of the Modern Public Episode 12: The News Revolution and the 18th Century Public Sphere." *Ideas*. CBC, 16 June 2010. *iTunes Podcasts*. Web. 1 September 2010.

Cayley, David. "The Origins of the Modern Public Episode 13: Publics and Counterpublics." *Ideas*. CBC. 23 June 2010. *iTunes Podcasts*. Web. 1 September 2010.

Cayley, David. "The Origins of the Modern Public Episode 14: The Public Sphere Today." *Ideas*. CBC. 30 June 2010. *iTunes Podcasts*. Web. 1 September 2010.

Chakravorty, Swapan. *Society and Politics in the Plays of Thomas Middleton*. Oxford: Oxford University Press, 1996.

Cherry, Caroline L. *The Most Unvaluedst Purchase: Women in the Plays of Thomas Middleton*. Lewiston: Edwin Mellen Press, 1973.

Clare, Janet. *"Art Made Tongue-Tied by Authority": Elizabethan and Jacobean Dramatic Censorship.* 2nd edition. Manchester: Manchester University Press, 1999.

Clare, Janet. "Censorship and Negotiation." In *Literature and Censorship in Renaissance England.* Edited by Andrew Hadfield. New York: Palgrave, 2001. 17–30.

Clark, Sandra. *The Elizabethan Pamphleteers.* London: Athlone Press, 1982.

Clegg, Cyndia S. *Press Censorship in Jacobean England.* Cambridge: Cambridge University Press, 2001.

Cogswell, Thomas. *The Blessed Revolution: English Politics and the Coming of War, 1621–1624.* Cambridge: Cambridge University Press, 1989.

Cogswell, Thomas. "The People's Love: The Duke of Buckingham and Popularity." In *Politics, Religion and Popularity in Early Stuart Britain.* Edited by Thomas Cogswell, Richard Cust, and Peter Lake. Cambridge: Cambridge University Press, 2002. 211–34.

Cogswell, Thomas. "Thomas Middleton and the Court, 1624: *A Game at Chess* in Context." *Huntington Library Quarterly* 47 (1984): 273–88.

Cogswell, Thomas, Richard Cust, and Peter Lake, eds. *Politics, Religion and Popularity in Early Stuart Britain.* Cambridge: Cambridge University Press, 2002.

Cogswell, Thomas, and Peter Lake. "Buckingham Does the Globe: *Henry VIII* and the Politics of Popularity in the 1620s." *Shakespeare Quarterly* 60, no. 3 (2009): 253–78.

Cooley, R. W. "Speech versus Spectacle: Autolycus, Class and Containment in *The Winter's Tale.*" *Renaissance and Reformation* 21, no. 3 (1997): 5–24.

Cox, Lee S. "The Role of Autolycus in *The Winter's Tale.*" *SEL* 9, no. 2 (1969): 283–301.

Cressy, David. "Literacy in Seventeenth-Century England." *Journal of Interdisciplinary History* 8 (1977): 144–64.

Cressy, David. *Travesties and Transgressions in Tudor and Stuart England: Tales of Discord and Dissension.* Oxford: Oxford University Press, 2000.

Croft, Pauline. *King James.* New York: Palgrave Macmillan, 2003.

Cross, Robert. "Pretense and Perception in the Spanish Match, or History in a Fake Beard." *Journal of Interdisciplinary History* 37 (2007): 563–83.

Crossley, Nick, and John M. Roberts. *After Habermas: New Perspectives on the Public Sphere.* Oxford: Blackwell, 2004.

Cruz, Anne J., ed. *Material and Symbolic Circulation between Spain and England, 1554–1604.* Aldershot: Ashgate, 2008.

Cust, Richard. "Charles I and Popularity." In *Politics, Religion and Popularity in Early Stuart Britain: Essays in Honour of Conrad Russell.* Edited by Thomas Cogswell, Richard Cust, and Peter Lake. Cambridge: Cambridge University Press, 2002. 235–58.

Cust, Richard. "News and Politics in Early Seventeenth-Century England." *Past and Present* 112 (1986): 60–90.

Cust, Richard, and Ann Hughes, eds. *Conflict in Early Stuart England: Studies in Religion and Politics, 1603–1642.* New York: Longman, 1989.

Cvetkovich, Ann. *Depression: A Public Feeling.* Durham: Duke University Press, 2012.

Dahl, Folke. "Amsterdam—Cradle of English Newspapers." *The Library.* 5th series 4, no. 3 (1949): 166–78.

Dahl, Folke. *A Bibliography of English Corantos and Periodical Newsbooks, 1620–1642.* London: Bibliographical Society, 1952.

Darby, Trudi L. "The Black Knight's Festival Book? Thomas Middleton's *A Game at Chess.*" In *The Spanish Match: Prince Charles's Journey to Madrid, 1623.* Edited by Alexander Samson. London: Ashgate, 2006. 173–88.

Davies, R. A., and A. R. Young. "Strange Cunning in Thomas Middleton's *A Game at Chess.*" *University of Toronto Quarterly* 45 (1976): 236–45.

Dawson, Anthony, and Paul Yachnin. *The Culture of Playgoing in Shakespeare's England: A Collaborative Debate.* Cambridge: Cambridge University Press, 2001.

Dooley, Brendan, and Sabrina A. Baron. *The Politics of Information in Early Modern Europe.* London: Routledge, 2001.

Donne, John. *The Variorum Edition of the Poetry of John Donne.* Edited by Gary A. Stringer. Bloomington: Indiana University Press, 1995.

Dutton, Richard. Introduction. "*A Game at Chess.*" In Thomas Middleton, *"Women Beware Women" and Other Plays.* Oxford: Oxford University Press, 1999. vii–xli.

Dutton, Richard. *Mastering the Revels: The Regulation and Censorship of English Renaissance Drama.* Iowa City: University of Iowa Press, 1991.

Dutton, Richard. "Receiving Offense: *A Game at Chess* Again." In *Literature and Censorship in Renaissance England.* Edited by Andrew Hadfield. New York: Palgrave, 2001. 50–74.

Eccles, Mark. "Thomas Gainsford, Captain Pamphlet." *Huntington Library Quarterly* 45, no. 4 (1982): 259–70.

Edwards, Philip, et al. *The Revels History of Drama in English,* volume 4: *1613–1660.* London: Methuen, 1981.

Engle, Lars. *Shakespearean Pragmatism: Market of His Time.* Chicago: University of Chicago Press, 1993.

Ettinghausen, Henry. "The Greatest News since the Resurrection? Andrés de Almansa y Mendoza's Coverage of Prince Charles's Spanish Trip." In *The Spanish Match: Prince Charles's Journey to Madrid, 1623.* Edited by Alexander Samson. London: Ashgate, 2006. 75–90.

Ewbank, Inga-Stina, "The Triumph of Time in *The Winter's Tale.*" *Review of English Literature* 5 (1964): 83–100.

Farmer, Alan B. "Play-Reading, News-Reading, and Ben Jonson's *The Staple of News.*" In *The Book of the Play: Playwrights, Stationers, and Readers in Early Modern England.* Edited by Marta Straznicky. Amherst: University of Massachusetts Press, 2006. 127–58.

Fleck, Andrew. "Vulgar Fingers of the Multitude: Shakespeare, Jonson, and the Transformation of News from the Low Countries." *Shakespeare Yearbook* 15 (2005): 89–111.

Frank, Joseph. *The Beginnings of the English Newspaper 1620–1660.* Cambridge, MA: Harvard University Press, 1961.

Friedman, Jerome. *The Battle of the Frogs and Fairford's Flies: Miracles and the Pulp Press during the English Revolution.* New York: St. Martin's Press, 1993.

Fuchs, Barbara. "Middleton and Spain." In *The Oxford Handbook of Thomas Middleton.* Edited by Gary Taylor and Trish T. Henley. Oxford: Oxford University Press, 2012. 404–17.

Gosson, Stephen. *The Schoole of Abuse, Conteining a Pleasunt Inuective Against Poets Pipers, Plaiers, Jesters and such like Catterpillers of a Commonwealth (1579).* Edited by Edward Arber. London: English Reprints, 1868.

Gras, Henk. "The Elizabethan Theatre as Early Modern Television." In *News and Politics in Early Modern Europe (1500–1800).* Edited by Joop W. Koopmans. Leuven: Peeters, 2005. 115–30.

Griffin, Eric. *English Renaissance Drama and the Specter of Spain.* Philadelphia: University of Pennsylvania Press, 2009.

Guilbault, Reta. "National Unity and English (Dis)Honour: Thomas Middleton's *A Game at Chess.*" *English Studies in Canada* 28, nos. 3–4 (2002): 355–84.

Gurr, Andrew. "London's Blackfriars Playhouse and the Chamberlain's Men." In *Inside Shakespeare: Essays on the Blackfriars Stage*. Edited by Paul Menzer. Selinsgrove: Susquehanna University Press, 2006. 17–34.

Gurr, Andrew. *Playgoing in Shakespeare's London*. Cambridge: Cambridge University Press, 1987.

Gurr, Andrew. *The Shakespearean Stage, 1574–1642*. Cambridge: Cambridge University Press, 1970.

Habermas, Jürgen. *The Structural Transformation of the Public Sphere: An Inquiry Into a Category of Bourgeois Society*. Translated by Thomas Burger. Cambridge, MA: MIT Press, 1989.

Hadfield, Andrew. "Introduction: The Politics of Early Modern Censorship." In *Literature and Censorship in Renaissance England*. Edited by Andrew Hadfield. New York: Palgrave, 2001. 1–16.

Hadfield, Andrew, ed. *Literature and Censorship in Renaissance England*. New York: Palgrave, 2001.

Halasz, Alexandra. *The Marketplace of Print: Pamphlets and the Public Sphere in Early Modern England*. Cambridge: Cambridge University Press, 1997.

Harrison, Jackie. *News*. London: Routledge, 2006.

Hartley, John. *Understanding News*. London: Methuen, 1982.

Heinemann, Margot. *Puritanism and Theatre: Thomas Middleton and Opposition Drama under the Early Stuarts*. Cambridge: Cambridge University Press, 1980.

Heller, Herbert Jack. *Penitent Brothellers: Grace, Sexuality, and Genre in Thomas Middleton's City Comedies*. Newark: University of Delaware Press, 2000.

Holdsworth, R. V. "Sexual Puns in Middleton, Chapman, and Dekker." *Notes & Queries* 229 (1984): 242–47.

Howard-Hill, T. H. *Middleton's "Vulgar Pasquin": Essays on "A Game at Chess"*. Newark: University of Delaware Press, 1995.

Howard-Hill, T. H. "Political Interpretations of Middleton's *A Game at Chess* (1624)." *Yearbook of English Studies* 21 (1991): 274–85.

Howard-Hill, T. H. "The Unique Eye-Witness Report of Middleton's *A Game at Chess*." *Review of English Studies* 42 (1991): 168–78.

Howell, Tom, and Nicola Luksic. "The Theatre of News." *Ideas*. CBC Radio. Original broadcast 23 June 2014.

Hughes, Paul L., and James F. Larkin, eds. *Tudor Royal Proclamations*. New Haven: Yale University Press 1969.

Israel, Jonathan I. *The Dutch Republic and the Hispanic World, 1606–1661*. Oxford: Clarendon Press, 1982.

Jones, Ann Rosalind, and Peter Stallybrass. *Renaissance Clothing and the Materials of Memory*. Cambridge: Cambridge University Press, 2000.

Jowett, Garth, and Victoria O'Donnell. *Propaganda and Persuasion*. Newbury Park: Sage Publications, 1986.

Jowett, John. *Shakespeare and Text*. Oxford: Oxford University Press, 2007.

Jowett, John. Introduction. "*Measure for Measure*." In Thomas Middleton, *The Collected Works*. Oxford: Clarendon, 2007. 1542–46.

Jowett, John. Introduction. "*Women Beware Women*." In Thomas Middleton, *The Collected Works*. Oxford: Clarendon, 2007. 1488–92.

Jowitt, Claire. "'I Am Another Woman': The Spanish and French Matches in Massinger's *The Renegado* (1624) and *The Unnatural Combat* (1624–5)." In *The Spanish Match: Prince Charles's Journey to Madrid, 1623*. Edited by Alexander Samson. London: Ashgate, 2006. 151–72.

Jowitt, Claire. *Voyage Drama and Gender Politics, 1589–1642: Real and Imagined Worlds.* Manchester: Manchester University Press, 2003.

Kamps, Ivo. *Historiography and Ideology in Stuart Drama.* Cambridge: Cambridge University Press, 1996.

Kastan, David, and Peter Stallybrass. *Staging the Renaissance: Reinterpretations of Elizabethan and Jacobean Drama.* New York: Routledge, 1991.

Keene, Nicholas, and Evelyn B. Tribble. *Cognitive Ecologies and the History of Remembering: Religion, Education and Memory in Early Modern England.* Houndmills: Palgrave Macmillan, 2011.

Kishlansky, Mark A. *A Monarchy Transformed: Britain, 1603–1714.* London: Penguin, 1996.

Kishlansky, Mark A. *Parliamentary Selection: Social and Political Choice in Early Modern England.* Cambridge: Cambridge University Press, 1986.

Kitch, Aaron. "Bastards and Broadsides in *The Winter's Tale.*" *Renaissance Drama* 30 (1999/2001): 43–71.

Lake, P. G. "Constitutional Consensus and Puritan Opposition in the 1620s: Thomas Scott and the Spanish Match." *Historical Journal* 25, no. 4 (1982): 805–25.

Lake, P. G. "Deeds against Nature: Cheap Print, Protestantism and Murder in Early Seventeenth-Century England." In *Culture and Politics in Early Stuart England.* Edited by Kevin Sharpe and Peter Lake. Stanford: Stanford University Press, 1993. 228–83.

Lake, Peter, and Michael C. Questier. *The Antichrist's Lewd Hat: Protestants, Papists and Players in Post-Reformation England.* New Haven: Yale University Press, 2002.

Lake, Peter, and Steven C. A. Pincus, eds. *The Politics of the Public Sphere in Early Modern England.* Manchester: Manchester University Press, 2007.

Lamb, Mary Ellen. "Engendering the Narrative Act: Old Wives' Tales in *The Winter's Tale, Macbeth,* and *The Tempest.*" *Criticism* 40 (1998): 529–55.

Lavagnino, John, and Gary Taylor, eds. *Thomas Middleton: The Collected Works.* Oxford: Clarendon, 2007.

Lavagnino, John, and Gary Taylor. *Thomas Middleton and Early Modern Textual Culture: A Companion to the Collected Works.* Oxford: Clarendon, 2007.

Lesser, Zachary. *Renaissance Drama and the Politics of Publication: Readings in the English Book Trade.* Cambridge: Cambridge University Press, 2004.

Levin, Richard. "*The Staple of News,* the Society of Jeerers, and Canters' College." *Philological Quarterly* 44 (1965): 445–53.

Levy, F. J. "The Decorum of News." In *News, Newspapers, and Society in Early Modern Britain.* Edited by Joad Raymond. Portland: Frank Cass, 1999. 12–38.

Levy, F. J. "How Information Spread among the Gentry, 1550–1640." *Journal of British Studies* 21, no. 2 (1982): 11–34.

Levy-Navarro, Elena. *The Culture of Obesity in Early and Late Modernity: Body Image in Shakespeare, Jonson, Middleton, and Skelton.* New York: Palgrave Macmillan, 2008.

Limon, Jerzy. *Dangerous Matter: English Drama and Politics in 1623–24.* Cambridge: Cambridge University Press, 1986.

Love, Harold. *Scribal Publication in Seventeenth-Century England.* Oxford: Clarendon, 1993.

Loewenstein, Joseph. *Ben Jonson and Possessive Authorship.* Cambridge: Cambridge University Press, 2002.

Lublin, Robert I. "'An Vnder Black Dublett Signifying a Spanish Hart': Costumes and Politics in Middleton's *A Game at Chess.*" *Theatre Survey* 48 (2007): 247–63.

Malcolmson, Christina. "'As Tame as the Ladies': Politics and Gender in *The Changeling.*" *English Literary Renaissance* 20, no. 2 (1990): 320–39.

McKenzie, D. F. "*The Staple of News* and the Late Plays." In *A Celebration of Ben Jonson*. Edited by William Blisset, Julian Patrick, and R. W. van Fossen. Toronto: University of Toronto Press, 1972. 83–128.

McShane-Jones. "*The Gazet in Metre; Or The Rhiming Newsmonger:* The English Broadside Ballad as Intelligencer. A New Narrative." In *News and Politics in Early Modern Europe (1500–1800)*. Edited by Joop W. Koopmans. Leuven: Peeters, 2005. 131–51.

Milgate, Wesley, ed. 1967. *John Donne: The Satires, Epigrams and Verse Letters*. Oxford: Clarendon Press, 1967.

Moore, J. R. "The Contemporary Significance of Middleton's *A Game at Chess*." *PMLA* 50 (1935): 761–68.

Morris, E. C. "The Allegory in Middleton's *A Game at Chess*." *Englische Studien* 38 (1907): 39–52.

Mowat, Barbara A. "Rogues, Shepherds, and the Counterfeit Distressed: Texts and Infracontexts of *The Winter's Tale* 4.3." *Shakespeare Studies* 22 (1994): 58–76.

Muggli, Mark Z. "Ben Jonson and the Business of News." *SEL* 32, no. 2 (1992): 323–40.

Mullaney, Steven. *The Place of the Stage: License, Play, and Power in Renaissance England*. Chicago: University of Chicago Press, 1988.

Mullaney, Steven. "Affective Technologies: Toward an Emotional Logic of the Elizabethan Stage." In *Environment and Embodiment in Early Modern England*. Edited by Mary Floyd-Wilson and Garrett Sullivan. Basingstoke: Palgrave Macmillan, 2007. 71–89.

Mullaney, Steven. "What's Hamlet to Habermas? Spatial Literacy, Theatrical Publication and the Publics of the Early Modern Public Stage." In *Making Space Public in Early Modern Europe: Performance, Geography, Privacy*. Edited by Angela Vanhaelen and Joseph P. Ward. New York: Routledge, 2013. 17–40.

Munro, Ian. "Making Publics: Secrecy and Publication in *A Game at Chess*." *Medieval and Renaissance Drama in England* 14 (2001): 207–26.

Nelson, Carolyn, and Matthew Seccombe. "The Creation of the Periodical Press 1620–1695." In *The Cambridge History of the Book in Britain*. Edited by John Barnard, D. F. McKenzie, and Maureen Bell. 5 vols. Cambridge: Cambridge University Press, 2002. Vol. 4, 533–50.

Nelson, Richard Alan. *A Chronology and Glossary of Propaganda in the United States*. Westport: Greenwood Press, 1996.

Nevitt, Marcus. "Ben Jonson and the Serial Publication of News." *Media History* 11 (2005): 53–68.

O'Callaghan, Michelle. *Thomas Middleton, Renaissance Dramatist*. Edinburgh: Edinburgh University Press, 2009.

O'Connor, Marion. Introduction. *The Witch*. In Thomas Middleton, *The Collected Works*. Oxford: Clarendon, 2007. 1124–64.

Orlin, Lena Cowen. *Private Matters and Public Culture in Post-Reformation England*. Ithaca: Cornell University Press, 1994.

Orgel, Stephen. "Marginal Jonson." In *The Politics of the Stuart Court Masque*. Edited by David Bevington and Peter Holbrook. Cambridge: Cambridge University Press, 1998. 144–75.

Paster, Gail Kern. *The Body Embarrassed: Drama and the Disciplines of Shame in Early Modern England*. Ithaca: Cornell University Press, 1993.

Paster, Gail Kern. *The Idea of the City in the Age of Shakespeare*. Athens: University of Georgia Press, 1985.

Patterson, Annabel M. *Censorship and Interpretation: The Conditions of Writing and Reading in Early Modern England.* Madison: University of Wisconsin Press, 1984.

Patterson, Annabel. Introduction. "*The Changeling.*" In Thomas Middleton, *The Collected Works.* Oxford: Clarendon, 2007. 1632–36.

Peck, Linda Levy, ed. *The Mental World of the Jacobean Court.* Cambridge: Cambridge University Press, 1991.

Peterson, Russell. "Strange Bedfellows: The Politics of Late-Night Television Comedy." *Poroi* 5, no. 1 (2008): 61–83.

Pettegree, Andrew. *The Invention of News: How the World Came to Know about Itself.* New Haven: Yale University Press, 2014.

Pitcher, John. "Some Call Him Autolycus." In *In Arden: Editing Shakespeare: Essays in Honour of Richard Proudfoot.* Edited by Ann Thompson and Gordon McMullan. London: Arden Shakespeare, 2003.

Price, G. R. "The Latin Oration in *A Game at Chess.*" *Huntington Library Quarterly* 23 (1960): 389–93.

Raymond, Joad. *The Invention of the Newspaper: English Newsbooks, 1641–1649.* Oxford: Clarendon Press, 1996.

Raymond, Joad, ed. *News, Newspapers, and Society in Early Modern Britain.* Portland: Frank Cass, 1999.

Raymond, Joad, ed. *News Networks in the Seventeenth-Century Britain and Europe.* London: Routledge, 2006.

Raymond, Joad. *Pamphlets and Pamphleteering in Early Modern Britain.* Cambridge: Cambridge University Press, 2003.

Redworth, Glyn. *The Prince and the Infanta: The Cultural Politics of the Spanish Match.* New Haven: Yale University Press, 2003.

Rockwood, Catherine. "Know Thy Side: Propaganda and Parody in Jonson's *Staple of News.*" *ELH* 75, no. 1 (2008): 135–49.

Rogers, H. L. "An English Tailor and Father Garnet's Straw." *Review of English Studies* 16, no. 61 (1965): 44–49.

Rollins, Hyder E. "The Black-Letter Broadside Ballad." *PMLA* 34, no. 2 (1919): 258–339.

Rose, Mary Beth. *The Expense of Spirit: Love and Sexuality in English Renaissance Drama.* Ithaca: Cornell University Press, 1988.

Rowen, Herbert H. *The Princes of Orange: The Stadholders in the Dutch Republic.* Cambridge: Cambridge University Press, 1988.

Salingar, L. G. "Time and Art in Shakespeare's Romances." *Renaissance Drama* 9 (1966): 3–35.

Samson, Alexander. "Introduction: The Spanish Match." In *The Spanish Match: Prince Charles's Journey to Madrid, 1623.* Edited by Alexander Samson. London: Ashgate, 2006. 1–8.

Samson, Alexander. "1623 and the Politics of Translation." In *The Spanish Match: Prince Charles's Journey to Madrid, 1623.* Edited by Alexander Samson. London: Ashgate, 2006. 91–106.

Sanders, Julie. *Ben Jonson's Theatrical Republics.* New York: St. Martin's Press, 1998.

Sanders, Julie. "Print, Popular Culture, Consumption and Commodification in *The Staple of News.*" In *Refashioning Ben Jonson: Gender, Politics, and the Jonsonian Canon.* Edited by Julie Sanders, Kate Chedgzoy, and Susan Wiseman. New York: St. Martin's Press, 1998. 183–207.

Sargent, Roussel. "Theme and Structure in Middleton's *A Game at Chess.*" *Modern Language Review* 66 (1971): 721–30.

Schalkwyk, David. "A Lady's 'Verily' Is as Potent as a Lord's: Women, Word and Witchcraft in *The Winter's Tale.*" *English Literary Renaissance* 22, no. 2 (1992): 242–72.

Shaaber, M. A. *Some Forerunners of the Newspaper in England, 1476–1622*. Philadelphia: University of Pennsylvania Press, 1929.

Sharpe, J. A. "'Last Dying Speeches': Religion, Ideology and Public Execution in Seventeenth-Century England." *Past & Present* 107 (1985): 144–67.

Sharpe, Kevin. *Reading Revolutions: The Politics of Reading in Early Modern England.* New Haven: Yale University Press, 2000.

Sharpe, Kevin. *Remapping Early Modern England: The Culture of Seventeenth-Century Politics.* Cambridge: Cambridge University Press, 2000.

Sharpe, Kevin, and Peter Lake. *Culture and Politics in Early Stuart England.* Stanford: Stanford, 1993.

Sherman, Jane. "The Pawns' Allegory in Middleton's *A Game at Chess.*" *Review of English Studies* 29 (1978): 147–59.

Sherman, Stuart. "Eyes and Ears, News, and Plays: The Argument of Ben Jonson's *Staple.*" In *The Politics of Information in Early Modern Europe.* Edited by Brendan M. Dooley and Sabrina A. Baron. London: Routledge, 2001. 23–40.

Shohet, Lauren. *Reading Masques: The English Masque and Public Culture in the Seventeenth Century.* Oxford: Oxford University Press, 2010.

Simmons, J. L. "Diabolical Realism in Middleton and Rowley's *The Changeling.*" *Renaissance Drama* 11 (1980): 135–70.

Simmons, Judith. "Publications of 1623." *The Library* 5th series 11, no. 3 (1966): 207–22.

Sisson, Charles J. *Lost Plays of Shakespeare's Age.* Cambridge: Cambridge University Press, 1936.

Smith, A. J., ed. *The Complete English Poems of John Donne.* Harmondsworth: Penguin, 1971.

Smith, Irwin. *Shakespeare's Blackfriars Playhouse: Its History and Its Design.* New York: New York University Press, 1964.

Stephens, Mitchell. *A History of News: From the Drum to the Satellite.* New York: Viking, 1988.

Taylor, Gary. *Castration: An Abbreviated History of Western Manhood.* New York: Routledge, 2000.

Taylor, Gary. "*A Game at Chess*: General Textual Introduction." In *Thomas Middleton and Early Modern Textual Culture: A Companion to the Collected Works.* Edited by John Lavagnino and Gary Taylor. Oxford: Clarendon, 2007. 712–873.

Taylor, Gary. Introduction. "*A Game at Chesse:* An Early Form." In Thomas Middleton, *The Collected Works.* Oxford: Clarendon, 2007. 1773–79.

Taylor, Gary. Introduction. "*A Game at Chesse:* A Later Form." In Thomas Middleton, *The Collected Works.* Oxford: Clarendon, 2007. 1825–29.

Turner, Olga, and E. W. Wilson. "The Spanish Protest against *A Game at Chess.*" *Modern Language Review* 44 (1949): 476–82.

Tribble, Evelyn. "Genius on the Rack: Authorities and the Margin in Ben Jonson's Glossed Works." *Exemplaria* 4, no. 2 (1992): 317–39.

Vanhaelen, Angela, and Joseph P. Ward, eds. *Making Space Public in Early Modern Europe: Performance, Geography, Privacy.* New York: Routledge, 2013.

Vaughan, Alden T. "William Strachey's 'True Reportory' and Shakespeare: A Closer Look at the Evidence." *Shakespeare Quarterly* 59, no. 3 (2008): 245–73.

Voss, Paul J. *Elizabethan News Pamphlets: Shakespeare, Spenser, Marlowe and the Birth of Journalism.* Pittsburgh: Duquesne University Press, 2001.

Walsham, Alexandra. *Providence in Early Modern England.* Oxford: Oxford University Press, 1999.

Warner, Michael. *Publics and Counterpublics.* New York: Zone Books, 2002.

Warner, Michael. "Publics and Counterpublics." *Quarterly Journal of Speech* 88 (2002): 413–25.

Watt, Tessa. *Cheap Print and Popular Piety, 1550–1640.* Cambridge: Cambridge University Press, 1991.

Welch, Kate. "Making Mourning Show: *Hamlet* and Affective Public-Making." *Performance Research* 16, no. 2 (2011): 74–82.

Wells, Marion. "Mistress Taleporter and the Triumph of Time: Slander and Old Wives' Tales in *The Winter's Tale.*" *Shakespeare Survey* 58 (2005): 247–59.

Wiggins, Martin. *Journeymen in Murder: The Assassin in English Renaissance Drama.* Oxford: Clarendon, 1991.

Wiggins, Martin. *Shakespeare and the Drama of His Time.* Oxford: Oxford University Press, 2000.

Wilson, Bronwen, and Paul Yachnin. *Making Publics in Early Modern Europe: People, Things, Forms of Knowledge.* New York: Routledge, 2010.

Woolf, Daniel. "News, History, and the Construction of the Present in Early Modern England." In *The Politics of Information in Early Modern Europe.* Edited by Brendan M. Dooley and Sabrina A. Baron. London: Routledge, 2001. 80–118.

Würzbach, Natascha. *The Rise of the English Street Ballad, 1550–1650.* Cambridge: Cambridge University Press, 2010.

Yachnin, Paul. "*A Game at Chess* and Chess Allegory." *SEL* 22, no. 2 (1982): 317–30.

Yachnin, Paul. "*A Game at Chess:* Thomas Middleton's *Praise of Folly.*" *Modern Language Quarterly* 48 (1987): 107–23.

Yachnin, Paul. "*Hamlet* and the Social Thing in Early Modern England." In *Making Publics in Early Modern Europe: People, Things, Forms of Knowledge.* Edited by Bronwen Wilson and Paul Yachnin. New York: Routledge, 2010. 81–95.

Yachnin, Paul. "A New Source for Middleton's *A Game at Chess.*" *Notes & Queries* 27, no. 2 (1980): 157–58.

Yachnin, Paul. "'The Perfection of Ten': Populuxe Art and Artisanal Value in *Troilus and Cressida.*" *Shakespeare Quarterly* 56, no. 3 (2006): 306–27.

Yachnin, Paul. "Performing Publicity." *Shakespeare Bulletin* 28, no. 2 (2010): 201–19.

Yachnin, Paul. "Playing with Space: Making A Public in Middleton's Theatre." In *The Oxford Handbook of Thomas Middleton.* Edited by Gary Taylor and Trish T. Henley. Oxford: Oxford University Press, 2012. 32–46.

Yachnin, Paul. "The Powerless Theater: Populuxe Art and Artisanal Value in *Troilus and Cressida.*" *English Literary Renaissance* 21, no. 1 (1991): 49–74.

Yachnin, Paul. *Stage-Wrights: Shakespeare, Jonson, Middleton, and the Making of Theatrical Value.* Philadelphia: University of Pennsylvania Press, 1997.

Zaret, David. *Origins of Democratic Culture: Printing, Petitions, and the Public Sphere in Early-Modern England.* Princeton: Princeton University Press, 2000.

Zimmerman, Susan. *Erotic Politics: Desire on the Renaissance Stage.* New York: Routledge, 1992.

Index